Workshop on Predicting and Improving Text Readability for Target Reader Populations 2013

Sofia, Bulgaria
8 August 2013

ISBN: 978-1-62748-988-1

Printed from e-media with permission by:

Curran Associates, Inc.
57 Morehouse Lane
Red Hook, NY 12571

Some format issues inherent in the e-media version may also appear in this print version.

Printed by Curran Associates, Inc. (2013)

For permission requests, please contact the Association for Computational Linguistics
at the address below.

Association for Computational Linguistics
209 N. Eighth Street
Stroudsburg, Pennsylvania 18360

Phone: 1-570-476-8006
Fax: 1-570-476-0860

acl@aclweb.org

Additional copies of this publication are available from:

Curran Associates, Inc.
57 Morehouse Lane
Red Hook, NY 12571 USA
Phone: 845-758-0400
Fax: 845-758-2634
Email: curran@proceedings.com
Web: www.proceedings.com

Introduction

Welcome to the second International Workshop on Predicting and Improving Text Readability for Target Reader Populations (PITR).

The last few years have seen a resurgence of work on text simplification and readability. Examples include learning lexical and syntactic simplification operations from Simple English Wikipedia revision histories, exploring more complex lexico-syntactic simplification operations requiring morphological changes as well as constituent reordering, simplifying mathematical form, applications for target users such as deaf students, second language learners and low literacy adults, and fresh attempts at predicting readability.

The PITR 2013 workshop has been organised to provide a cross-disciplinary forum for discussing key issues related to predicting and improving text readability for target users. It will be held on August 8, 2013 in conjunction with the 51st Conference of the Association for Computational Linguistics in Sofia, Bulgaria, and is sponsored by the ACL Special Interest Group on Speech and Language Processing for Assistive Technologies (SIG-SLPAT).

These proceedings include nine papers that cover various perspectives on the topic. Papers this year fall into 3 broad categories: (i) Readability Enhancement, where the aim is to improve text quality in some way (e.g., inserting punctuation) or tailor text for specific users (e.g., hearing-impaired readers); (ii) Predicting the reading level of text, where approaches vary from psycho-linguistic measurements (e.g. reading time) to standard readability measures applied to particular genres (e.g., web texts); and (iii) Text Simplification, where papers address learning from corpora as well as evaluation metrics for simplification systems.

We hope this volume is a valuable addition to the literature, and look forward to an exciting Workshop.

Sandra Williams
Advaith Siddharthan
Ani Nenkova

Organizers:

Sandra Williams, The Open University, UK.
Advaith Siddharthan, University of Aberdeen, UK.
Ani Nenkova, University of Pennsylvania, USA.

Program Committee:

Julian Brooke, University of Toronto, Canada.
Kevyn Collins-Thompson, Microsoft Research (Redmond), USA.
Siobhan Devlin, University of Sunderland, UK.
Micha Elsner, University of Edinburgh, UK.
Thomas François, University of Louvain, Belgium.
Caroline Gasperin, TouchType Ltd., UK.
Albert Gatt, University of Malta, Malta.
Pablo Gervás, Universidad Complutense de Madrid, Spain.
Iryna Gurevych, Technische Universitat Darmstadt, Germany.
Raquel Hervás, Universidad Complutense de Madrid, Spain.
Véronique Hoste, University College Ghent, Belgium.
Matt Huenerfauth, The City University of New York (CUNY), USA.
Iustina Ilisei, University of Wolverhampton, UK.
Annie Louis, University of Pennsylvania, USA.
Hitoshi Nishikawa, NTT, Japan.
Ehud Reiter, University of Aberdeen, UK.
Horacio Saggion, Universitat Pompeu Fabra, Spain.
Irina Temnikova, University of Wolverhampton, UK.
Ielka van der Sluis, University of Groningen, The Netherlands.
Kristian Woodsend, University of Edinburgh, UK.

Invited Speaker:

Annie Louis, University of Edinburgh, UK.

Identifying outstanding writing: Corpus and experiments based on the science journalism genre

I will discuss the hitherto unexplored area of text quality prediction: identifying outstanding pieces of writing. A system to do this task will benefit article recommendation and information retrieval. To do the task, we need to not only be able to measure spelling, grammar and organization quality but also quantify creative and engaging writing and topic. In addition, new resources are needed as existing corpora are focused on non-native student writing, output of text generation systems and artificial manipulation to create texts with low quality writing.

I will propose the science journalism genre as an apt one for such text quality experiments. Science journalism pieces entertain a reader as much as they teach and inform. I will introduce a corpus of science journalism articles which we have collected for use in text quality studies. The corpus contains science journalism pieces from the New York Times split into two categories—written by award-winning journalists and others. This corpus offers many desirable properties which were unavailable in previous resources. It represents realistic differences in writing quality, samples are based on professional writers rather than language learners, contains thousands of articles, and is publicly available. I will also describe automatic measures based on visual elements, surprisal and structure of these articles which are indicative of outstanding articles in the corpus and also turn out complementary to traditional metrics to quantify readability and organization quality of writing.

Bio: Annie Louis is a Newton International Fellow at the University of Edinburgh. She completed her PhD at University of Pennsylvania with a thesis on text quality prediction. She has also worked on automatic summarization and discourse parsing. She is currently working on discourse and document-level issues in machine translation. Annie has received a EMNLP best paper award and a SIGDIAL best student paper award.

Table of Contents

Workshop Program

(August 8, 2013)

09:20 – 10.30 **Session 1: Plenary**

09:20 Welcome and Introduction

09:30 Invited Talk: *Identifying outstanding writing: Corpus and experiments based on the science journalism genre*
Annie Louis, University of Edinburgh

10:30 – 11.00 Coffee break

11:00 – 12.30 **Session 2: Posters**

11:00 Poster Teasers

11:20 Poster Session

Sentence Simplification as Tree Transduction
Dan Feblowitz and David Kauchak

Building a German/Simple German Parallel Corpus for Automatic Text Simplification
David Klaper, Sarah Ebling and Martin Volk

The C-Score – Proposing a Reading Comprehension Metrics as a Common Evaluation Measure for Text Simplification
Irina Temnikova and Galina Maneva

A Language-Independent Approach to Automatic Text Difficulty Assessment for Second-Language Learners
Wade Shen, Jennifer Williams, Tamas Marius and Elizabeth Salesky

Guest paper: *A System for the Simplification of Numerical Expressions at Different Levels of Understandability*
Susana Bautista, Raquel Hervás, Pablo Gervás, Richard Powerand Sandra Williams (2013). Proc. Workshop on NLP for Improving Textual Accessibility (NLP4ITA), Atlanta, USA, pp.10–19.

12:30 – 14:00 Lunch break

14:00 – 15:30	**Session 3: Presentations**

14:00 *Text Modification for Bulgarian Sign Language Users*
Slavina Lozanova, Ivelina Stoyanova, , Svetlozara Leseva, , Svetla Koeva and Boian Savtchev

14:20 *Modeling Comma Placement in Chinese Text for Better Readability using Linguistic Features and Gaze Information*
Tadayoshi Hara, Chen Chen, Yoshinobu Kano and Akiko Aizawa

14:40 *On The Applicability of Readability Models to Web Texts*
Sowmya Vajjala and Detmar Meurers

15:00 *Report from NLP4ITA 2013*
Horacio Saggion

15:20 – 16:00	Tea break

16:00 – 1700	**Session 4: Presentations and Close**

16:00 *The CW Corpus: A New Resource for Evaluating the Identification of Complex Words*
Matthew Shardlow

16:20 *A Pilot Study of Readability Prediction with Reading Time*
Hitoshi NISHIKAWA, Toshiro MAKINO and Yoshihiro MATSUO

16:50 Final Discussion and Close

Sentence Simplification as Tree Transduction

Dan Feblowitz
Computer Science Department
Pomona College
Claremont, CA
djf02007@mymail.pomona.edu

David Kauchak
Computer Science Department
Middlebury College
Middlebury, VT
dkauchak@middlebury.edu

Abstract

In this paper, we introduce a syntax-based sentence simplifier that models simplification using a probabilistic synchronous tree substitution grammar (STSG). To improve the STSG model specificity we utilize a multi-level backoff model with additional syntactic annotations that allow for better discrimination over previous STSG formulations. We compare our approach to T3 (Cohn and Lapata, 2009), a recent STSG implementation, as well as two state-of-the-art phrase-based sentence simplifiers on a corpus of aligned sentences from English and Simple English Wikipedia. Our new approach performs significantly better than T3, similarly to human simplifications for both simplicity and fluency, and better than the phrase-based simplifiers for most of the evaluation metrics.

1 Introduction

Text simplification is aimed at reducing the reading and grammatical complexity of text while retaining the meaning. Text simplification has applications for children, language learners, people with disabilities (Carroll et al., 1998; Feng, 2008) and in technical domains such as medicine (Elhadad, 2006), and can be beneficial as a preprocessing step for other NLP applications (Vickrey and Koller, 2008; Miwa et al., 2010). In this paper we introduce a new probabilistic model for sentence simplification using synchronous tree substitution grammars (STSG).

Synchronous grammars can be viewed as simultaneously generating a pair of recursively related strings or trees (Chiang, 2006). STSG grammar rules contain pairs of tree fragments called *elementary trees* (Eisner, 2003; Cohn and Lapata, 2009; Yamangil and Shieber, 2010). The leaves of an elementary tree can be either terminal, lexical nodes or aligned *nonterminals* (also referred to as variables or frontier nodes). Because elementary trees may have any number of internal nodes structured in any way STSGs allow for more complicated derivations not expressible with other synchronous grammars.

To simplify an existing tree, an STSG grammar is used as a tree transducer. Figure 1 shows some example simplification STSG rules written in transductive form. As a transducer the grammar rules take an elementary tree and rewrite it as the tree on the right-hand side of the rule. For example, the first rule in Figure 1 would make the transformation

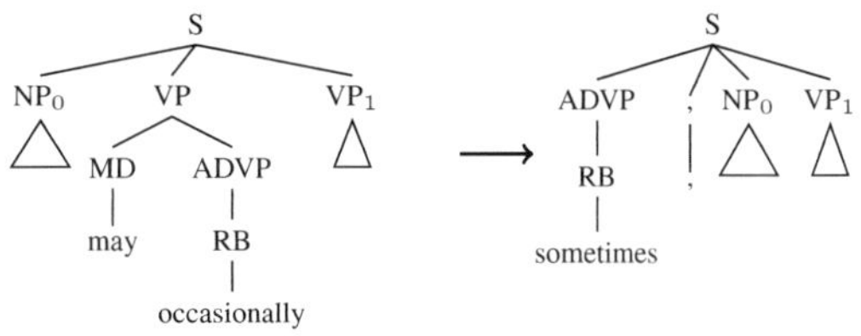

changing "may occasionally" to "sometimes ," and moving the noun phrase from the beginning of the sentence to after the comma. The indices on the nonterminals indicate alignment and transduction continues recursively on these aligned nonterminals until no nonterminals remain. In the example above, transduction would continue down the tree on the NP and VP subtrees. A probabilistic STSG has a probability associated with each rule.

One of the key challenges in learning an STSG from an aligned corpus is determining the right level of specificity for the rules: too general and they can be applied in inappropriate contexts; too specific, and the rules do not apply in enough contexts. Previous work on STSG learning has regulated the rule specificity based on elementary tree depth (Cohn and Lapata, 2009), however, this approach has not worked well for text simplifica-

S(NP$_0$ VP(MD(may) ADVP(RB(occasionally))) VP$_1$)	$\rightarrow$	S(ADVP(RB(sometimes)) ,(,) NP$_0$ VP$_1$)
NP(NNS$_0$)	$\rightarrow$	NP(NNS$_0$)
NP(JJ$_0$ NNS$_1$)	$\rightarrow$	NP(JJ$_0$ NNS$_1$)
VP(VB$_0$ PP(IN(in) NP$_1$))	$\rightarrow$	VP(VB$_0$ NP$_1$)
VB(assemble),	$\rightarrow$	VB(join)
JJ(small)	$\rightarrow$	JJ(small)
NNS(packs)	$\rightarrow$	NNS(packs)
NNS(jackals)	$\rightarrow$	NNS(jackals)

Figure 1: Example STSG rules representing the maximally general set for the aligned trees in Figure 2. The rules are written in transductive form. Aligned nonterminals are indicated by indices.

tion (Coster and Kauchak, 2011a). In this paper, we take a different approach and augment the grammar with additional information to increase the specificity of the rules (Galley and McKeown, 2007). We combine varying levels of grammar augmentation into a single probabilistic backoff model (Yamangil and Nelken, 2008). This approach creates a model that uses specific rules when the context has been previously seen in the training data and more general rules when the context has not been seen.

2 Related Work

Our formulation is most closely related to the T3 model (Cohn and Lapata, 2009), which is also based on the STSG formalism. T3 was developed for the related problem of text compression, though it supports the full range of transformation operations required for simplification. We use a modified version of their constituent alignment and rule extraction algorithms to extract the basic STSG rules with three key changes. First, T3 modulates the rule specificity based on elementary tree depth, while we use additional grammar annotations combined via a backoff model allowing for a broader range of context discrimination. Second, we learn a probabilistic model while T3 learns the rule scores discriminatively. T3's discriminative training is computationally prohibitive for even modest sized training sets and a probabilistic model can be combined with other probabilities in a meaningful way. Third, our implementation outputs an n-best list which we then rerank based on a trained log-linear model to select the final candidate.

Zhu et al. (2010) suggest a probabilistic, syntax-based approach to text simplification. Unlike the STSG formalism, which handles all of the transformation operations required for sentence simplification in a unified framework, their model uses a combination of hand-crafted components, each designed to handle a different transformation operation. Because of this model rigidity, their system performed poorly on evaluation metrics that take into account the content and relative to other simplification systems (Wubben et al., 2012).

Woodsend and Lapata (2011) introduce a quasi-synchronous grammar formulation and pose the simplification problem as an integer linear program. Their model has similar representational capacity to an STSG, though the learned models tend to be much more constrained, consisting of $<$1000 rules. With this limited rule set, it is impossible to model all of the possible lexical substitutions or to handle simplifications that are strongly context dependent. This quasi-synchronous grammar approach performed better than Zhu et al. (2010) in a recent comparison, but still performed worse than recent phrase-based approaches (Wubben et al., 2012).

A number of other approaches exist that use Simple English Wikipedia to learn a simplification model. Yatskar et al. (2010) and Biran et al. (2011) learn lexical simplifications, but do not tackle the more general simplification problem. Coster and Kauchak (2011a) and Wubben et al. (2012) use a modified phrase-based model based on a machine translation framework. We compare against both of these systems. Qualitatively, we find that phrasal models do not have the representative power of syntax-based approaches and tend to only make small changes when simplifying.

Finally, there are a few early rule-based simplification systems (Chandrasekar and Srinivas, 1997; Carroll et al., 1998) that provide motivation for recent syntactic approaches. Feng (2008) provides a good overview of these.

3 Probabilistic Tree-to-Tree Transduction

We model text simplification as tree-to-tree transduction with a probabilistic STSG acquired from

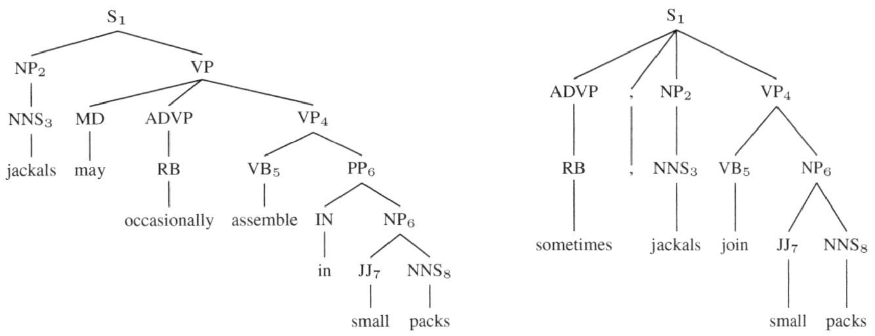

Figure 2: An example pair of constituent aligned trees generated by the constituent alignment algorithm. Aligned constituents are indicated with a shared index number (e.g. NP_2 is aligned to NP_2).

a parsed, sentence-aligned corpus between normal and simplified sentences. To learn the grammar, we first align tree constituents based on an induced word alignment then extract grammar rules that are consistent with the constituent alignment. To improve the specificity of the grammar we augment the original rules with additional lexical and positional information. To simplify a sentence based on the learned grammar, we generate a finite-state transducer (May and Knight, 2006) and use the transducer to generate an n-best list of simplifications. We then rerank the n-best list of simplifications using a trained log-linear model and output the highest scoring simplification. The subsections below look at each of these steps in more detail. Throughout the rest of this paper, we will refer to the unsimplified text/trees as *normal* and the simplified variants as *simple*.

3.1 Rule Extraction

Given a corpus of pairs of trees representing normal and simplified sentences, the first step is to extract a set of basic STSG production rules from each tree pair. We used a modified version of the algorithm presented by Cohn and Lapata (2009). Due to space constraints, we only present here a brief summary of the algorithm along with our modifications to the original algorithm. See Cohn and Lapata (2009) for more details.

Word-level alignments are learned using Giza++ (Och and Ney, 2000) then tree nodes (i.e. constituents) are aligned if: there exists at least one pair of nodes below them that is aligned *and* all nodes below them are either aligned to a node under the other constituent or unaligned. Given the constituent alignment, we then extract the STSG production rules. Because STSG rules can have arbitrary depth, there are often many possible sets of rules that could be extracted from a pair of trees.[1] Following Cohn and Lapata (2009) we extract the *maximally general* rule set from an aligned pair of input trees that is consistent with the alignment: the set of rules capable of synchronously deriving the original aligned tree pair consisting of rules with the smallest depth. Figure 2 shows an example tree pair that has been constituent aligned and Figure 1 shows the extracted STSG rules.

We modify the constituent alignment algorithm from Cohn and Lapata (2009) by adding the requirement that if node b with parent a are both aligned to node z and its parent y, we only align the pairs (a, y) and (b, z), i.e. align the children and align the parents. This eliminates a common occurrence where too many associations are made between a pair of preterminal nodes and their children. For example, for the sentences shown in Figure 2 the word alignment contains "`assemble`" aligned to "`join`". Under the original definition four aligned pairs would be generated:

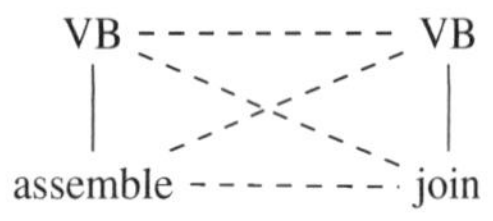

but only two under our revised definition:

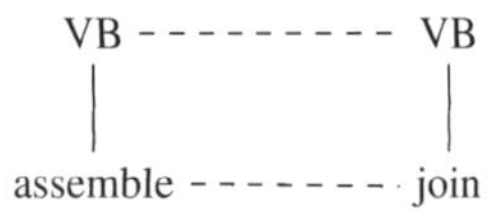

This revised algorithm reduces the size of the alignment, decreasing the number of cases which must be checked during grammar extraction while preserving the intuitive correspondence.

[1]There is always at least one set of rules that can generate a tree pair consisting of the entire trees.

3.2 Grammar Generation

During the production rule extraction process, we select the production rules that are most general. More general rules allow the resulting transducer to handle more potential inputs, but can also result in unwanted transformations. When generating the grammar, this problem can be mitigated by also adding more specific rules.

Previous approaches have modulated rule specificity by incorporating rules of varying depth in addition to the maximally general rule set (Cohn and Lapata, 2009), though this approach can be problematic. Consider the aligned subtrees rooted at nodes (VP_4, VP_4) in Figure 2. An STSG learning algorithm that controls rule specificity based on depth must choose between generating the rule:

$VP(VB_0\ PP(IN(in)\ NP_1)) \rightarrow VP(VB_0\ NP_1)$

which drops the preposition, or a deeper rule that includes the lexical leaves such as:

$VP(VB(assemble)\ PP(IN(in)\ NP_1)) \rightarrow VP(VB(join)\ NP_1)$

or

$VP(VB(assemble)\ PP(IN(in)\ NP(JJ_0\ NNS_1))) \rightarrow$
$VP(VB(join)\ NP(JJ_0\ NNS_1))$

If either of the latter rule forms is chosen, the applicability is strongly restricted because of the specificity and lexical requirement. If the former rule is chosen and we apply this rule we could make the following inappropriate transformation:

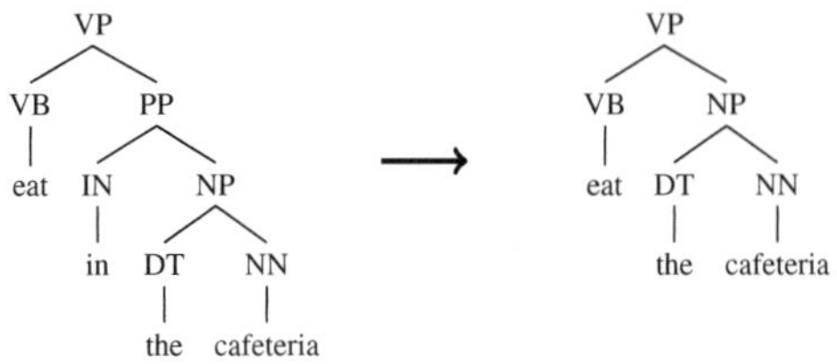

simplifying *"eat in the cafeteria"* to *"eat the cafeteria"*.

We adopt a different approach to increase the rule specificity. We augment the production rules and resulting grammar with several parse tree annotations shown previously to improve SCFG-based sentence compression (Galley and McKeown, 2007) as well as parsing (Collins, 1999): parent annotation, head-lexicalization, and annotation with the part of speech of the head word.

Following Yamangil and Nelken (2008), we learn four different models and combine them into a single backoff model. Each model level increases specificity by adding additional rule annotations. Model 1 contains only the original production rules. Model 2 adds parent annotation, Model 3 adds the head child part of speech and Model 4 adds head child lexicalization. The head child was determined using the set of rules from Collins (1999). Figure 3 shows the four different model representations for the VP rule above.

3.3 Probability Estimation

We train each of the four models individually using maximum likelihood estimation over the training corpus, specifically:

$$p(s|n) = \frac{count(s \wedge n)}{count(n)}$$

where s and n are tree fragments with that level's annotation representing the right and left sides of the rule respectively.

During simplification, we start with the most specific rules, i.e. Model 4. If a tree fragment was not observed in the training data at that model level, we repeatedly try a model level simpler until a model is found with the tree fragment (Yamangil and Nelken, 2008). We then use the probability distribution given by that model. A tree fragment only matches at a particular level if all of the annotation attributes match for all constituents. If none of the models contain a given tree fragment we introduce a rule that copies the tree fragment with probability one.

Two types of out-of-vocabulary problems can occur and the strategy of adding copy rules provides robustness against both. In the first, an input contains a tree fragment whose structure has never been seen in training. In this case, copy rules allow the structure to be reproduced, leaving the system to make more informed changes lower down in the tree. In the second, the input contains an unknown word. This only affects transduction at the leaves of the tree since at the lower backoff levels nodes are not annotated with words. Adding copy rules allows the program to retain, replace, or delete unseen words based only on the probabilities of rules higher up for which it does have estimates. In both cases, the added copy rules make sure that any input tree will have an output.

3.4 Decoding and Reranking

Given a parsed sentence to simplify and the probabilistic STSG grammar, the last step is to find the most likely transduction (i.e. simplification) of the input tree based on the grammar. To accomplish this, we convert the STSG grammar into an equivalent finite tree-to-tree transducer: each STSG

Model 1:	VP (VB_0 PP (IN(in) NP_1)) → VP (VB_0 NP_1)
Model 2:	VP^VP (VB^VP_0 PP^VP (IN^PP (in) NP^PP_1)) → VP^S (VB^VP_0 NP^VP_1)
Model 3:	VP[VB]^VP (VB^VP_0 PP[NNS]^VP (IN^PP (in) NP[NNS]^PP_1)) → VP[VB]^S (VB^VP_0 NP[NNS]^VP_1)
Model 4:	VP[VB-assemble]^VP (VB[assemble]^VP_0 PP[NNS-packs]^VP (IN[in]^PP (in) NP[NNS-packs]^PP_1)) → VP[VB-join]^S (VB[join]^VP_0 NP[NNS-packs]^VP_1)

Figure 3: The four levels of rule augmentation for an example rule ranging from Model 1 with no additional annotations to Model 4 with all annotations. The head child and head child part of speech are shown in square brackets and the parent constituent is annotated with ^.

grammar rule represents a state transition and is weighted with the grammar rule's probability. We then use the Tiburon tree automata package (May and Knight, 2006) to apply the transducer to the parsed sentence. This yields a weighted regular tree grammar that generates every output tree that can result from rewriting the input tree using the transducer. The probability of each output tree in this grammar is equal to the product of the probabilities of all rewrite rules used to produce it.

Using this output regular tree grammar and Tiburon, we generate the 10,000 most probable output trees for the input parsed sentence. We then rerank this candidate list based on a log-linear combination of features:

- The simplification probability based on the STSG backoff model.
- The probability of the output tree's yield, as given by an n-gram language model trained on the simple side of the training corpus using the IRSTLM Toolkit (Federico et al., 2008).
- The probability of the sequence of the part of speech tags in the output tree, as given by an n-gram model trained on the part of speech tags of the simple side of the training corpus.
- A two-sided length penalty decreasing the score of output sentences whose length, normalized by the length of the input, deviates from the training corpus mean, found empirically to be 0.85.

The first feature represents the simplification likelihood based on the STSG grammar described above. The next two features ensure that outputs are well-formed according to the language used in Simple English Wikipedia. Finally, the length penalty is used to prevent both over-deletion and over-insertion of out-of-source phrases. In addition, the length feature mean could be reduced or increased to encourage shorter or longer simplifications if desired.

The weights of the log-linear model are optimized using random-restart hill-climbing search (Russell and Norvig, 2003) to maximize BLEU (Papineni et al., 2002) on a development set.[2]

4 Experiment Setup

To train and evaluate the systems we used the data set from Coster and Kauchak (2011b) consisting of 137K aligned sentence pairs between Simple English Wikipedia and English Wikipedia. The sentences were parsed using the Berkeley Parser (Petrov and Klein, 2007) and the word alignments determined using Giza++ (Och and Ney, 2000). We used 123K sentence pairs for training, 12K for development and 1,358 for testing.

We compared our system (**SimpleTT** – simple tree transducer) to three other simplification approaches:

T3: Another STSG-based approach (Cohn and Lapata, 2009). Our approach shares similar constituent alignment and rule extraction algorithms, but our approach differs in that it is generative instead of discriminative, and T3 increases rule specificity by increasing rule depth, while we employ a backoff model based on grammar augmentation. In addition, we employ n-best reranking based on a log-linear model that incorporates a number of additional features.

The code for T3 was obtained from the authors.[3] Due to performance limitations, T3 was only trained on 30K sentence pairs. T3 was run on the full training data for two weeks, but it never terminated and required over 100GB of memory. The slow algorithmic step is the discriminative training, which cannot be easily parallelized. T3 was tested for increasing amounts of data up to

[2]BLEU was chosen since it has been used successfully in the related field of machine translation, though this approach is agnostic to evaluation measure.

[3]`http://staffwww.dcs.shef.ac.uk/people/T.Cohn/t3/`

30K training pairs and the results on the automatic evaluation measures did not improve.

Moses-Diff: A phrase-based approach based on the Moses machine translation system (Koehn et al., 2007) that selects the simplification from the 10-best output list that is most *different* from the input sentence (Wubben et al., 2012). Moses-Diff has been shown to perform better than a number of recent syntactic systems including Zhu et al. (2010) and Woodsend and Lapata (2011).

Moses-Del: A phrase-based approach also based on Moses which incorporates phrasal deletion (Coster and Kauchak, 2011b). The code was obtained from the authors.

For an additional data point to understand the benefit of the grammar augmentation, we also evaluated a deletion-only system previously used for text compression and a variant of that system that included the grammar augmentation described above. **K&M** is a synchronous context free grammar-based approach (Knight and Marcu, 2002) and **augm-K&M** adds the grammar augmentation along with the four backoff levels.

There are currently no standard evaluation metrics for text simplification. Following previous work (Zhu et al., 2010; Coster and Kauchak, 2011b; Woodsend and Lapata, 2011; Wubben et al., 2012) we evaluated the systems using automatic metrics to analyze different system characteristics and human evaluations to judge the system quality.

Automatic Evaluation

- *BLEU* (Papineni et al., 2002): BLEU measures the similarity between the system output and a human reference and has been used successfully in machine translation. Higher BLEU scores are better, indicating an output that is more similar to the human reference simplification.
- *Oracle BLEU*: For each test sentence we generate the 1000-best output list and greedily select the entry with the highest sentence-level BLEU score. We then calculate the BLEU score over the entire test set for all such greedily selected sentences. The oracle score provides an analysis of the generation capacity of the model and gives an estimate of the upper bound on the BLEU score attainable through reranking.
- *Length ratio*: The ratio of the length of the original, unsimplified sentence and the system simplified sentence.

Human Evaluation

Following previous work (Woodsend and Lapata, 2011; Wubben et al., 2012) we had humans judge the three simplification systems and the human simplifications from Simple English Wikipedia (denoted **SimpleWiki**)[4] based on three metrics: simplicity, fluency and adequacy. Simplicity measures how simple the output is, fluency measures the quality of the language and grammatical correctness of the output, and adequacy measures how well the content is preserved. For the fluency experiments, the human evaluators were just shown the system output. For simplicity and adequacy, in addition to the system output, the original, unsimplified sentence was also shown. All metrics were scored on a 5-point Likert scale with higher indicating better.

We used Amazon's Mechanical Turk (MTurk)[5] to collect the human judgements. MTurk has been used by many NLP researchers, has been shown to provide results similar to other human annotators and allows for a large population of annotators to be utilized (Callison-Burch and Dredze, 2010; Gelas et al., 2011; Zaidan and Callison-Burch, 2011).

We randomly selected 100 sentences from the test set where all three systems made some change to the input sentence. We chose sentences where all three systems made a change to focus on the *quality* of the simplifications made by the systems. For each sentence we collected scores from 10 judges, for each of the systems, for each of the three evaluation metrics (a total of 100*10*3*3 = 9000 annotations). The scores from the 10 judges were averaged to give a single score for each sentence and metric. Judges were required to be within the U.S. and have a prior acceptance rate of 95% or higher.

5 Results

Automatic evaluation

Table 1 shows the results of the automatic evaluation metrics. SimpleTT performs significantly better than T3, the other STSG-based model, and obtains the second highest BLEU score behind only Moses-Del. SimpleTT has the highest oracle BLEU score, indicating that the syntactic model of SimpleTT allows for more diverse simplifications

[4]T3 was not included in the human evaluation due to the very poor quality of the output based on both the automatic measures and based on a manual review of the output.

[5]https://www.mturk.com/

System	BLEU	Oracle	Length Ratio
SimpleTT	0.564	**0.663**	0.849
Moses-Diff	0.543	–*	0.960
Moses-Del	**0.605**	0.642	0.991
T3	0.244	–**	0.581
K&M	0.406	0.602	0.676
augm-K&M	0.498	0.609	0.826
corpus mean	–	–	0.85

Table 1: Automatic evaluation scores for all systems tested and the mean values from the training corpus. *Moses-Diff uses the n-best list to choose candidates and therefore is not amenable to oracle scoring. **T3 only outputs the single best simplification.

	simplicity	fluency	adequacy
SimpleWiki	3.45	3.93	3.42
SimpleTT	3.55	3.80	3.09
Moses-Diff	3.07	3.64	3.91
Moses-Del	3.19	3.74	3.86

Table 2: Human evaluation scores on a 5-point Likert scale averaged over 100 sentences.

than the phrase-based models and may be more amenable to future reranking techniques. SimpleTT also closely matches the in-corpus mean of the length ratio seen by human simplifications, though this can be partially explained by the length penalty in the log-linear model.

Moses-Del obtains the highest BLEU score, but accomplishes this with only small changes to the input sentence: the length of the simplified sentences are only slightly different from the original (a length ratio of 0.99). Moses-Diff has the lowest BLEU score of the three simplification systems and while it makes larger changes than Moses-Del it still makes much smaller changes than SimpleTT and the human simplifications.

T3 had significant problems with over-deleting content as indicated by the low length ratio which resulted in a very low BLEU score. This issue has been previously noted by others when using T3 for text compression (Nomoto, 2009; Marsi et al., 2010).

The two deletion-only systems performed worse than the three simplification systems. Comparing the two systems shows the benefit of the grammar augmentation: augm-K&M has a significantly higher BLEU score than K&M and also avoided the over-deletion that occurred in the original K&M system. The additional specificity of the rules allowed the model to make better decisions for which content to delete.

Human evaluation

Table 2 shows the human judgement scores for the simplification approaches for the three different metrics averaged over the 100 sentences and Table 3 shows the pairwise statistical significance calculations between each system based on a two-tailed paired t-test. Overall, SimpleTT performed well with simplicity and fluency scores that were comparable to the human simplifications. SimpleTT was too aggressive at removing content, resulting in lower adequacy scores. This phenomena was also seen in the human simplifications and may be able to be corrected in future variations by adjusting the sentence length target.

The human evaluations highlight the trade-off between the simplicity of the output and the amount of content preserved. For simplicity, SimpleTT and the human simplifications performed significantly better than both the phrase-based systems. However, simplicity does come with a cost; both SimpleTT and the human simplifications reduced the length of the sentences by 15% on average. This content reduction resulted in lower adequacy than the phrase-based systems. A similar trade-off has been previously shown for text compression, balancing content versus the amount of compression (Napoles et al., 2011).

For fluency, SimpleTT again scored similarly to the human simplifications. SimpleTT performed significantly better than Moses-Diff and slightly better than Moses-Del, though the difference was not statistically significant.

As an aside, Moses-Del performs slightly better than Moses-Diff overall. They perform similarly on adequacy and Moses-Del performs better on simplicity and Moses-Diff performs worse relative to the other systems on fluency.

Qualitative observations

SimpleTT tended to simplify by deleting prepositional, adjective, and adverbial phrases, and by truncating conjunctive phrases to one of their conjuncts. This often resulted in outputs that were syntactically well-formed with only minor information loss, for example, it converts

"The Haiti national football team is the national team of Haiti and is controlled by the Fédération Hatïenne de Football."

to

Simplicity

	SimpleWiki	Moses-Diff	Moses-Del
SimpleTT		$\Leftarrow\Leftarrow\Leftarrow$	$\Leftarrow\Leftarrow\Leftarrow$
SimpleWiki		$\Leftarrow\Leftarrow\Leftarrow$	$\Leftarrow\Leftarrow\Leftarrow$
Moses-Diff			$\Uparrow$

Fluency

	SimpleWiki	Moses-Diff	Moses-Del
SimpleTT		$\Leftarrow$	
SimpleWiki		$\Leftarrow\Leftarrow\Leftarrow$	$\Leftarrow$
Moses-Diff			

Adequacy

	SimpleWiki	Moses-Diff	Moses-Del
SimpleTT	$\Uparrow\Uparrow$	$\Uparrow\Uparrow\Uparrow$	$\Uparrow\Uparrow\Uparrow$
SimpleWiki		$\Uparrow\Uparrow\Uparrow$	$\Uparrow\Uparrow\Uparrow$
Moses-Diff			

Table 3: Pairwise statistical significance test results between systems for the human evaluations based on a paired t-test. The number of arrows denotes significance with one, two and three arrows indicating $p < 0.05$, $p < 0.01$ and $p < 0.001$ respectively. The direction of the arrow points towards the system that performed better.

> *"The Haiti national football team is the national football team of Haiti."*

which only differs from the human reference by one word.

SimpleTT also produces a number of interesting lexical and phrasal substitutions, including:

football striker	$\rightarrow$	*football player*
football defender	$\rightarrow$	*football player*
in order to	$\rightarrow$	*to*
known as	$\rightarrow$	*called*
member	$\rightarrow$	*part*

T3, on the other hand, tended to over-delete content, for example simplifying:

> *"In earlier times, they frequently lived on the outskirts of communities, generally in squalor."*

to just

> *"A lived".*

As we saw in the automatic evaluation results, the phrase-based systems tended to make fewer changes to the input and those changes it did make tended to be more minor. Moses-Diff was more aggressive about making changes, though it was more prone to errors since the simplifications chosen were more distant from the input sentence than other options in the n-best list.

6 Conclusions and Future work

In this paper, we have introduced a new probabilistic STSG approach for sentence simplification, SimpleTT. We improve upon previous STSG approaches by: 1) making the model probabilistic instead of discriminative, allowing for an efficient, unified framework that can be easily interpreted and combined with other information sources, 2) increasing the model specificity using four levels of grammar annotations combined into a single model, and 3) incorporating n-best list reranking combining the model score, language model probabilities and additional features to choose the final output. SimpleTT performs significantly better than previous STSG formulations for text simplification. In addition, our approach was rated by human judges similarly to human simplifications in both simplicity and fluency and it scored better than two state-of-the-art phrase-based sentence simplification systems along many automatic and human evaluation metrics.

There are a number of possible directions for extending the capabilities of SimpleTT and related systems. First, while some sentence splitting can occur in SimpleTT due to sentence split and merge examples in the training data, SimpleTT does not explicitly model this. Sentence splitting could be incorporated as another probabilistic component in the model (Zhu et al., 2010). Second, in this work, like many previous researchers, we assume Simple English Wikipedia as our target simplicity level. However, the difficulty of Simple English Wikipedia varies across articles and there are many domains where the desired simplicity varies depending on the target consumer. In the future, we plan to explore how varying algorithm parameters (for example the length target) affects the simplicity level of the output. Third, one of the benefits of SimpleTT and other probabilistic systems is they can generate an n-best list of candidate simplifications. Better reranking of output sentences could close this gap across all these systems, without requiring deep changes to the underlying model.

References

Or Biran, Samuel Brody, and Noemie Elhadad. 2011. Putting it simply: A context-aware approach to lexical simplification. In *Proceedings of ACL*.

Chris Callison-Burch and Mark Dredze. 2010. Creating speech and language data with Amazon's Mechanical Turk. In *Proceedings of NAACL-HLT Workshop on Creating Speech and Language Data with Amazon's Mechanical Turk.*

John Carroll, Gido Minnen, Yvonne Canning, Siobhan Devlin, and John Tait. 1998. Practical simplification of English newspaper text to assist aphasic readers. In *Proceedings of AAAI Workshop on Integrating AI and Assistive Technology.*

Raman Chandrasekar and Bangalore Srinivas. 1997. Automatic induction of rules for text simplification. In *Knowledge Based Systems.*

David Chiang. 2006. An introduction to synchronous grammars. Part of a tutorial given at ACL.

Trevor Cohn and Mirella Lapata. 2009. Sentence compression as tree transduction. *Journal of Artificial Intelligence Review.*

Michael Collins. 1999. *Head-Driven Statistical Models for Natural Language Parsing.* Ph.D. thesis, University of Pennsylvania.

William Coster and David Kauchak. 2011a. Learning to simplify sentences using Wikipedia. In *Proceedings of the Workshop on Monolingual Text-To-Text Generation.*

William Coster and David Kauchak. 2011b. Simple English Wikipedia: A new text simplification task. In *Proceedings of ACL.*

Jason Eisner. 2003. Learning non-isomorphic tree mappings for machine translation. In *Proceedings of ACL.*

Noemie Elhadad. 2006. Comprehending technical texts: predicting and defining unfamiliar terms. In *Proceedings of AMIA.*

Marcello Federico, Nicola Bertoldi, and Mauro Cettolo. 2008. IRSTLM: An open source toolkit for handling large scale language models. In *Proceedings of Interspeech*, Brisbane, Australia.

Lijun Feng. 2008. Text simplification: A survey. CUNY Technical Report.

Michel Galley and Kathleen McKeown. 2007. Lexicalized Markov grammars for sentence compression. In *Proceedings of HLT-NAACL.*

Hadrien Gelas, Solomon Teferra Abate, Laurent Besacier, and Francois Pellegrino. 2011. Evaluation of crowdsourcing transcriptions for African languages. In *Interspeech.*

Kevin Knight and Daniel Marcu. 2002. Summarization beyond sentence extraction: a probabilistic approach to sentence compression. *Artificial Intelligence.*

Philipp Koehn, Hieu Hoang, Alexandra Birch, Chris Callison-Burch, Marcello Federico, Nicola Bertoldi, Brooke Cowan, Wade Shen, Christine Moran, Richard Zens, Chris Dyer, Ondrej Bojar, Alexandra Constantin, and Evan Herbst. 2007. Moses: Open source toolkit for statistical machine translation. In *Proceedings of ACL.*

Erwin Marsi, Emiel Krahmer, Iris Hendrickx, and Walter Daelemans. 2010. On the limits of sentence compression by deletion. In *Empirical Methods in NLG.*

Jonathan May and Kevin Knight. 2006. Tiburon: A weighted tree automata toolkit. In *Proceedings of CIAA.*

Makoto Miwa, Rune Saetre, Yusuke Miyao, and Jun'ichi Tsujii. 2010. Entity-focused sentence simplification for relation extraction. In *Proceedings of COLING.*

Courtney Napoles, Benjamin Van Durme, and Chris Callison-Burch. 2011. Evaluating sentence compression: pitfalls and suggested remedies. In *Proceedings of the Workshop on Monolingual Text-To-Text Generation.*

Tadashi Nomoto. 2009. A comparison of model free versus model intensive approaches to sentence compression. In *Proceedings of EMNLP.*

Franz Och and Hermann Ney. 2000. Improved statistical alignment models. In *Proceedings of ACL.*

Kishore Papineni, Kishore Papineni, Salim Roukos, Salim Roukos, Todd Ward, Todd Ward, Wei jing Zhu, and Wei jing Zhu. 2002. BLEU: A method for automatic evaluation of machine translation. In *Proceedings of ACL.*

Slav Petrov and Dan Klein. 2007. Improved inference for unlexicalized parsing. In *Proceedings of HTL-NAACL.*

Stuart Russell and Peter Norvig. 2003. Artificial intelligence: A modern approach.

David Vickrey and Daphne Koller. 2008. Sentence simplification for semantic role labeling. In *Proceedings of ACL.*

Kristian Woodsend and Mirella Lapata. 2011. Learning to simplify sentences with quasi-synchronous grammar and integer programming. In *Proceedings of EMNLP.*

Sander Wubben, Antal van den Bosch, and Emiel Krahmer. 2012. Sentence simplification by monolingual machine translation. In *Proceedings of ACL.*

Elif Yamangil and Rani Nelken. 2008. Mining wikipedia revision histories for improving sentence compression. In *Proceedings of HLT-NAACL.*

Elif Yamangil and Stuart Shieber. 2010. Bayesian synchronous tree-substitution grammar induction and its application to sentence compression. In *Proceedings of ACL.*

Mark Yatskar, Bo Pang, Cristian Danescu-Niculescu-Mizil, and Lillian Lee. 2010. For the sake of simplicity: Unsupervised extraction of lexical simplifications from Wikipedia. In *Proceedings of HLT-NAACL.*

Omar F. Zaidan and Chris Callison-Burch. 2011. Crowdsourcing translation: Professional quality from non-professionals. In *Proceedings of ACL.*

Zhemin Zhu, Delphine Bernhard, and Iryna Gurevych. 2010. A monolingual tree-based translation model for sentence simplification. In *Proceedings of ICCL.*

Building a German/Simple German Parallel Corpus for Automatic Text Simplification

David Klaper **Sarah Ebling** **Martin Volk**
Institute of Computational Linguistics, University of Zurich
Binzmühlestrasse 14, 8050 Zurich, Switzerland
david.klaper@uzh.ch, {ebling|volk}@cl.uzh.ch

Abstract

In this paper we report our experiments in creating a parallel corpus using German/Simple German documents from the web. We require parallel data to build a statistical machine translation (SMT) system that translates from German into Simple German. Parallel data for SMT systems needs to be aligned at the sentence level. We applied an existing monolingual sentence alignment algorithm. We show the limits of the algorithm with respect to the language and domain of our data and suggest ways of circumventing them.

1 Introduction

Simple language (or, "plain language", "easy-to-read language") is language with low lexical and syntactic complexity. It provides access to information to people with cognitive disabilities (e.g., aphasia, dyslexia), foreign language learners, Deaf people,[1] and children. Text in simple language is obtained through *simplification*. Simplification is a text-to-text generation task involving multiple operations, such as deletion, rephrasing, reordering, sentence splitting, and even insertion (Coster and Kauchak, 2011a). By contrast, *paraphrasing* and *compression*, two other text-to-text generation tasks, involve merely rephrasing and reordering (paraphrasing) and deletion (compression). Text simplification also shares common ground with grammar and style checking as well as with controlled natural language generation.

Text simplification approaches exist for various languages, including English, French, Spanish, and Swedish. As Matausch and Nietzio (2012) write, "plain language is still underrepresented in the German speaking area and needs further development". Our goal is to build a statistical machine translation (SMT) system that translates from German into Simple German.

SMT systems require two corpora aligned at the sentence level as their training, development, and test data. The two corpora together can form a *bilingual* or a *monolingual* corpus. A bilingual corpus involves two different languages, while a monolingual corpus consists of data in a single language. Since text simplification is a text-to-text generation task operating within the same language, it produces monolingual corpora.

Monolingual corpora, like bilingual corpora, can be either *parallel* or *comparable*. A parallel corpus is a set of two corpora in which "a noticeable number of sentences can be recognized as mutual translations" (Tomás et al., 2008). Parallel corpora are often compiled from the publications of multinational institutions, such as the UN or the EU, or of governments of multilingual countries, such as Canada (Koehn, 2005). In contrast, a comparable corpus consists of two corpora created independently of each other from distinct sources. Examples of comparable documents are news articles written on the same topic by different news agencies.

In this paper we report our experiments in creating a monolingual parallel corpus using German/Simple German documents from the web. We require parallel data to build an SMT system that translates from German into Simple German. Parallel data for SMT systems needs to be aligned at the sentence level. We applied an existing monolingual sentence alignment algorithm. We show the limits of the algorithm with respect to the language and domain of our data and suggest ways of circumventing them.

The remainder of this paper is organized as follows: In Section 2 we discuss the methodologies pursued and the data used in previous work deal-

[1] It is an often neglected fact that Deaf people tend to exhibit low literacy skills (Gutjahr, 2006).

ing with automatic text simplification. In Section 3 we describe our own approach to building a German/Simple German parallel corpus. In particular, we introduce the data obtained from the web (Section 3.1), describe the sentence alignment algorithm we used (Section 3.2), present the results of the sentence alignment task (Section 3.3), and discuss them (Section 3.4). In Section 4 we give an overview of the issues we tackled and offer an outlook on future work.

2 Approaches to Text Simplification

The task of simplifying text automatically can be performed by means of rule-based, corpus-based, or hybrid approaches. In a rule-based approach, the operations carried out typically include replacing words by simpler synonyms or rephrasing relative clauses, embedded sentences, passive constructions, etc. Moreover, definitions of difficult terms or concepts are often added, e.g., the term *web crawler* is defined as "a computer program that searches the Web automatically". Gasperin et al. (2010) pursued a rule-based approach to text simplification for Brazilian Portuguese within the *PorSimples* project,[2] as did Brouwers et al. (2012) for French.

As part of the corpus-based approach, machine translation (MT) has been employed. Yatskar et al. (2010) pointed out that simplification is "a form of MT in which the two 'languages' in question are highly related".

As far as we can see, Zhu et al. (2010) were the first to use English/Simple English Wikipedia data for automatic simplification via machine translation.[3] They assembled a monolingual comparable corpus[4] of 108,016 sentence pairs based on the interlanguage links in Wikipedia and the sentence alignment algorithm of Nelken and Shieber (2006) (cf. Section 3.2). Their system applies a "tree-based simplification model" including machine translation techniques. The system learns probabilities for simplification operations (substitution, reordering, splitting, deletion) offline from the comparable Wikipedia data. At runtime, an input sentence is parsed and zero or more simplification operations are carried out based on the model probabilities.

Specia (2010) used the SMT system *Moses* (Koehn et al., 2007) to translate from Brazilian Portuguese into a simpler version of this language. Her work is part of the *PorSimples* project mentioned above. As training data she used 4483 sentences extracted from news texts that had been manually translated into Simple Brazilian Portuguese.[5] The results, evaluated automatically with BLEU (Papineni et al., 2002) and NIST (Doddington, 2002) as well as manually, show that the system performed lexical simplification and sentence splitting well, while it exhibited problems in reordering phrases and producing subject–verb–object (SVO) order. To further improve her system Specia (2010) suggested including syntactic information through hierarchical SMT (Chiang, 2005) and part-of-speech tags through factored SMT (Hoang, 2007).

Coster and Kauchak (2011a; 2011b) translated from English into Simple English using English/Simple English Wikipedia data. Like Specia (2010), they applied *Moses* as their MT system but in addition to the default configuration allowed for phrases to be empty. This was motivated by their observation that 47% of all Simple English Wikipedia sentences were missing at least one phrase compared to their English Wikipedia counterparts. Coster and Kauchak (2011a; 2011b) used four baselines to evaluate their system: input=output,[6] two text compression systems, and vanilla *Moses*. Their system, *Moses-Del*, achieved higher automatic MT evaluation scores (BLEU) than all of the baselines. In particular, it outperformed vanilla *Moses* (lacking the phrase deletion option).

Wubben et al. (2012) also worked with English/Simple English Wikipedia data and *Moses*. They added a post-hoc reranking step: Following their conviction that the output of a simplification system has to be a modified version of the input,[7] they rearranged the 10-best sentences output by *Moses* such that those differing from the

[2] `http://www2.nilc.icmc.usp.br/wiki/index.php/English`

[3] English Wikipedia: `http://en.wikipedia.org/`; Simple English Wikipedia: `http://simple.wikipedia.org/`.

[4] We consider this corpus to be comparable rather than parallel because not every Simple English Wikipedia article is necessarily a translation of an English Wikipedia article. Rather, Simple English articles can be added independently of any English counterpart.

[5] Hence, the corpus as a whole is a monolingual parallel corpus.

[6] The underlying assumption here was that not every sentence needs simplification.

[7] Note that this runs contrary to the assumption Coster and Kauchak (2011a; 2011b) made.

input sentences were given preference over those that were identical. Difference was calculated on the basis of the Levenshtein score (edit distance). Wubben et al. (2012) found their system to work better than that of Zhu et al. (2010) when evaluated with BLEU, but not when evaluated with the Flesch-Kincaid grade level, a common readability metric.

Bott and Saggion (2011) presented a monolingual sentence alignment algorithm, which uses a Hidden Markov Model for alignment. In contrast to other monolingual alignment algorithms, Bott and Saggion (2011) introduced a monotonicity restriction, i.e., they assumed the order of sentences to be the same for the original and simplified texts.

Apart from purely rule-based and purely corpus-based approaches to text simplification, hybrid approaches exist. For example, Bott et al. (2012) in their *Simplext* project for Spanish[8] let a statistical classifier decide for each sentence of a text whether it should be simplified (corpus-based approach). The actual simplification was then performed by means of a rule-based approach.

As has been shown, many MT approaches to text simplification have used English/Simple English Wikipedia as their data. The only exception we know of is Specia (2010), who together with her colleagues in the *PorSimples* project built her own parallel corpus. This is presumably because there exists no Simple Brazilian Portuguese Wikipedia. The same is true for German: To date, no Simple German Wikipedia has been created. Therefore, we looked for data available elsewhere for our machine translation system designated to translate from German to Simple German. We discovered that German/Simple German parallel data is slowly becoming available on the web. In what follows, we describe the data we harvested and report our experience in creating a monolingual parallel corpus from this data.

3 Building a German/Simple German Parallel Corpus from the Web

3.1 Data

As mentioned in Section 1, statistical machine translation (SMT) systems require parallel data. A common approach to obtain such material is to look for it on the web.[9] The use of already available data offers cost and time advantages. Many websites, including that of the German government,[10] contain documents in Simple German. However, these documents are often not linked to a single corresponding German document; instead, they are high-level summaries of multiple German documents.

A handful of websites exist that offer articles in two versions: a German version, often called *Alltagssprache* (AS, "everyday language"), and a Simple German version, referred to as *Leichte Sprache* (LS, "simple language"). Table 1 lists the websites we used to compile our corpus. The numbers indicate how many parallel articles were extracted. The websites are mainly of organizations that support people with disabilities. We crawled the articles with customized Python scripts that located AS articles and followed the links to their LS correspondents. A sample sentence pair from our data is shown in Example 1.

(1) **German:**
Wir freuen uns über Ihr Interesse an unserer Arbeit mit und für Menschen mit Behinderung.
("We appreciate your interest in our work with and for people with disabilities.")

Simple German:
Schön, dass Sie sich für unsere Arbeit interessieren.
Wir arbeiten mit und für Menschen mit Behinderung.
("Great that you are interested in our work. We work with and for people with disabilities.")

The extracted data needed to be cleaned from HTML tags. For our purpose, we considered text and paragraph structure markers as important information; therefore, we retained them. We subsequently tokenized the articles. The resulting corpus consisted of 7755 sentences, which amounted to 82,842 tokens. However, caution is advised when looking at these numbers: Firstly, the tokenization module overgenerated tokens. Secondly, some of the LS articles were identical, either because they summarized multiple AS articles or because they were generic placeholders. Hence, the

[8] http://www.simplext.es/

[9] Resnik (1999) was the first to discuss the possibility of collecting parallel corpora from the web.

[10] http://www.bundesregierung.de/Webs/Breg/DE/LeichteSprache/leichteSprache_node.html (last accessed 15th April 2013)

Short name	URL	No. of parallel art.
ET	`www.einfach-teilhaben.de`	51
GWW	`www.gww-netz.de`	65
HHO	`www.os-hho.de`	34
LMT	`www.lebenshilfe-main-taunus.de`	47
OWB	`www.owb.de`	59

Table 1: Websites and number of articles extracted

actual numbers were closer to 7000 sentences and 70,000 tokens.

SMT systems usually require large amount of training data. Therefore, this small experimental corpus is certainly not suitable for large-scale SMT experiments. However, it can serve as proof of concept for German sentence simplification. Over time more resources will become available.

SMT systems rely on data aligned at the sentence level. Since the data we extracted from the web was aligned at the article level only, we had to perform sentence alignment. For this we split our corpus into a training set (70% of the texts), development set (10%), and test set (20%). We manually annotated sentence alignments for all of the data. Example 2 shows an aligned AS/LS sentence pair.

(2) **German:**
In den Osnabrücker Werkstätten (OW) und OSNA-Techniken sind rund 2.000 Menschen mit einer Behinderung beschäftigt.
("In the Osnabrück factories and OSNA-Techniken, about 2.000 people with disability are employed.")

Simple German:
In den Osnabrücker Werkstätten und den Osna-Techniken arbeiten zweitausend Menschen mit Behinderung.
("Two thousand people with disability work in the Osnabrück factories and Osna-Techniken.")

To measure the amount of parallel sentences in our data, we calculated the *alignment diversity measure* (ADM) of Nelken and Shieber (2006). ADM measures how many sentences are aligned. It is calculated as $\frac{2*matches(T1,T2)}{|T1|+|T2|}$, where $matches$ is the number of alignments between the two texts $T1$ and $T2$. ADM is 1.0 in a perfectly parallel corpus, where every sentence from one text is aligned to exactly one sentence in another text.

ADM for our corpus was 0.786, which means that approximately 78% of the sentences were aligned. This is a rather high number compared to the values reported by Nelken and Shieber (2006): Their texts (consisting of encyclopedia articles and gospels) resulted in an ADM of around 0.3. A possible explanation for the large difference in ADM is the fact that most simplified texts in our corpus are solely based on the original texts, whereas the simple versions of the encyclopedia articles might have been created by drawing on external information in addition.

3.2 Sentence Alignment Algorithm

Sentence alignment algorithms differ according to whether they have been developed for bilingual or monolingual corpora. For bilingual parallel corpora many—typically length-based—algorithms exist. However, our data was monolingual. While the length of a regular/simple language sentence pair might be different, an overlap in vocabulary can be expected. Hence, monolingual sentence alignment algorithms typically exploit lexical similarity.

We applied the monolingual sentence alignment algorithm of Barzilay and Elhadad (2003). The algorithm has two main features: Firstly, it uses a hierarchical approach by assigning paragraphs to clusters and learning mapping rules. Secondly, it aligns sentences despite low lexical similarity if the context suggests an alignment. This is achieved through local sequence alignment, a dynamic programming algorithm.

The overall algorithm has two phases, a training and a testing phase. The training phase in turn consists of two steps: Firstly, all paragraphs of the texts of one side of the parallel corpus (henceforth referred to as "AS texts") are clustered independently of all paragraphs of the texts of the other side of the parallel corpus (henceforth termed "LS texts"), and vice versa. Secondly, mappings between the two sets of clusters are calculated, given the reference alignments.

As a preprocessing step to the clustering process, we removed stopwords, lowercased all words, and replaced dates, numbers, and names by generic tags. Barzilay and Elhadad (2003) additionally considered every word starting with a capital letter inside a sentence to be a proper name. In German, all nouns (i.e., regular nouns as well as proper names) are capitalized; thus, this approach does not work. We used a list of 61,228 first names to remove at least part of the proper names.

We performed clustering with scipy (Jones et al., 2001). We adapted the hierarchical complete-link clustering method of Barzilay and Elhadad (2003): While the authors claimed to have set a specific number of clusters, we believe this is not generally possible in hierarchical agglomerative clustering. Therefore, we used the largest number of clusters in which all paragraph pairs had a cosine similarity strictly greater than zero.

Following the formation of the clusters, lexical similarity between all paragraphs of corresponding AS and LS texts was computed to establish probable mappings between the two sets of clusters. Barzilay and Elhadad (2003) used the boosting tool Boostexter (Schapire and Singer, 2000). All possible cross-combinations of paragraphs from the parallel training data served as training instances. An instance consisted of the cosine similarity of the two paragraphs and a string combining the two cluster IDs. The classification result was extracted from the manual alignments. In order for an AS and an LS paragraph to be aligned, at least one sentence from the LS paragraph had to be aligned to one sentence in the AS paragraph. Like Barzilay and Elhadad (2003), we performed 200 iterations in Boostexter. After learning the mapping rules, the training phase was complete.

The testing phase consisted of two additional steps. Firstly, each paragraph of each text in the test set was assigned to the cluster it was closest to. This was done by calculating the cosine similarity of the word frequencies in the clusters. Then, every AS paragraph was combined with all LS paragraphs of the parallel text, and Boostexter was used in classification mode to predict whether the two paragraphs were to be mapped.

Secondly, within each pair of paragraphs mapped by Boostexter, sentences with very high lexical similarity were aligned. In our case, the threshold for an alignment was a similarity of 0.5. For the remaining sentences, proximity to other aligned or similar sentences was used as an indicator. This was implemented by local sequence alignment. We set the mismatch penalty to 0.02, as a higher mismatch penalty would have reduced recall. We set the skip penalty to 0.001 conforming to the value of Barzilay and Elhadad (2003). The resulting alignments were written to files. Example 3 shows a successful sentence alignment.

(3) **German:**
Die GWW ist in den Landkreisen Böblingen und Calw aktiv und bietet an den folgenden Standorten Wohnmöglichkeiten für Menschen mit Behinderung an – ganz in Ihrer Nähe!
("The GWW is active in the counties of Böblingen and Calw and offers housing options for people with disabilities at the following locations – very close to you!")

Simple German:
Die GWW gibt es in den Landkreisen Calw und Böblingen.
Wir haben an den folgenden Orten Wohn-Möglichkeiten für Sie.
("The GWW exists in the counties of Calw and Böblingen. We have housing options for you in the following locations.")

The algorithm described has been modified in various ways. Nelken and Shieber (2006) used TF/IDF instead of raw term frequency, logistic regression on the cosine similarity instead of clustering, and an extended version of the local alignment recurrence. Both Nelken and Shieber (2006) and Quirk et al. (2004) found that the first sentence of each document is likely to be aligned. We observed the same for our corpus. Therefore, in our algorithm we adopted the strategy of unconditionally aligning the first sentence of each document.

3.3 Results

Table 2 shows the results of evaluating the algorithm described in the previous section with respect to precision, recall, and F1 measure. We introduced two baselines:

Method	Precision	Recall	F1
Adapted algorithm of Barzilay and Elhadad (2003)	27.7%	5.0%	8.5%
Baseline I: First sentence	88.1%	4.8%	9.3%
Baseline II: Word in common	2.2%	8.2%	3.5%

Table 2: Alignment results on test set

1. Aligning only the first sentence of each text ("First sentence")
2. Aligning every sentence with a cosine similarity greater than zero ("Word in common")

As can be seen from Table 2, by applying the sentence alignment algorithm of Barzilay and Elhadad (2003) we were able to extract only 5% of all reference alignments, while precision was below 30%. The rule of aligning the first sentences performed well with a precision of 88%. Aligning all sentences with a word in common clearly showed the worst performance; this is because many sentences have a word in common. Nonetheless, recall was only slightly higher than with the other methods.

In conclusion, none of the three approaches (adapted algorithm of Barzilay and Elhadad (2003), two baselines "First sentence" and "Word in common") performed well on our test set. We analyzed the characteristics of our data that hampered high-quality automatic alignment.

3.4 Discussion

Compared with the results of Barzilay and Elhadad (2003), who achieved 77% precision at 55.8% recall for their data, our alignment scores were considerably lower (27.7% precision, 5% recall). We found two reasons for this: language challenges and domain challenges. In what follows, we discuss each reason in more detail.

While Barzilay and Elhadad (2003) aligned English/Simple English texts, we dealt with German/Simple German data. As mentioned in Section 3.2, in German nouns (regular nouns as well as proper names) are capitalized. This makes named entity recognition, a preprocessing step to clustering, more difficult. Moreover, German is an example of a morphologically rich language: Its noun phrases are marked with case, leading to different inflectional forms for articles, pronouns, adjectives, and nouns. English morphology is poorer; hence, there is a greater likelihood of lexical overlap. Similarly, compounds are productive in German; an example from our corpus is *Seniorenwohnanlagen* ("housing complexes for the elderly"). In contrast, English compounds are multiword units, where each word can be accessed separately by a clustering algorithm. Therefore, cosine similarity is more effective for English than it is for German. One way to alleviate this problem would be to use extensive morphological decomposition and lemmatization.

In terms of domain, Barzilay and Elhadad (2003) used city descriptions from an encyclopedia for their experiments. For these descriptions clustering worked well because all articles had the same structure (paragraphs about culture, sports, etc.). The domain of our corpus was broader: It included information about housing, work, and events for people with disabilities as well as information about the organizations behind the respective websites.

Apart from language and domain challenges we observed heavy transformations from AS to LS in our data (Figure 1 shows a sample article in AS and LS). As a result, LS paragraphs were typically very short and the clustering process returned many singleton clusters. Example 4 shows an AS/LS sentence pair that could not be aligned because of this.

(4) **German:**
Der Beauftragte informiert über die Gesetzeslage, regt Rechtsänderungen an, gibt Praxistipps und zeigt Möglichkeiten der Eingliederung behinderter Menschen in Gesellschaft und Beruf auf.
("The delegate informs about the legal situation, encourages revisions of laws, gives practical advice and points out possibilities of including people with disabilities in society and at work.")

Simple German:
Er gibt ihnen Tipps und Infos.

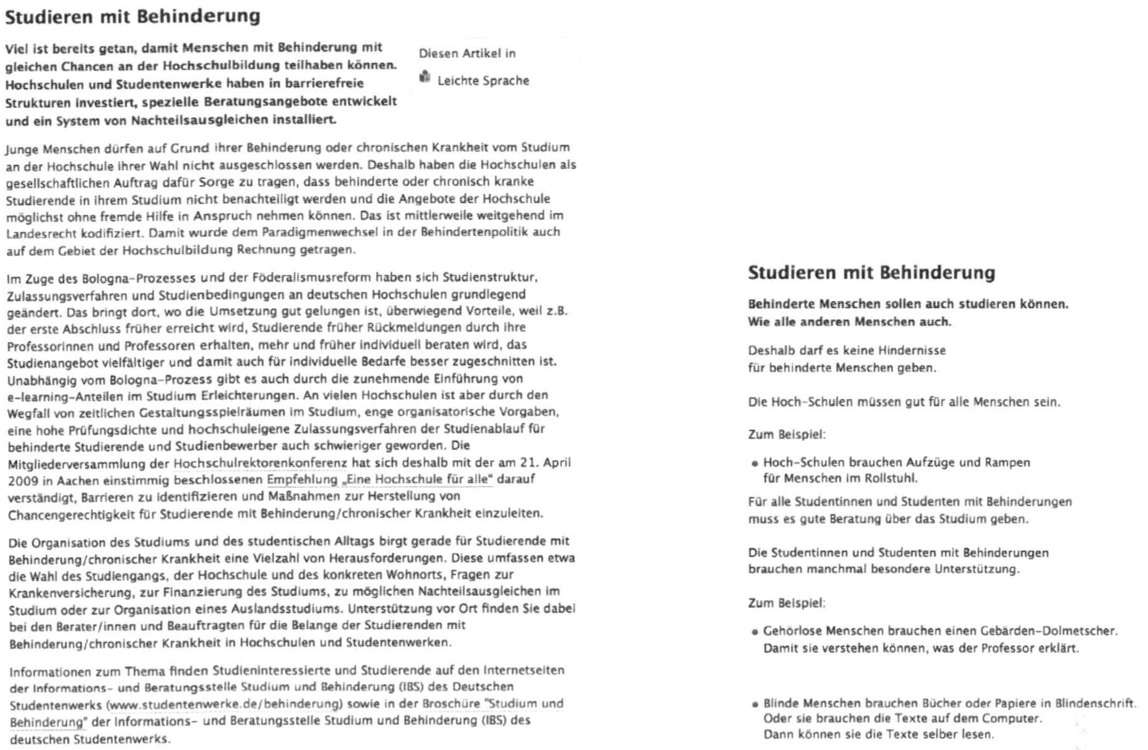
Studieren mit Behinderung

Viel ist bereits getan, damit Menschen mit Behinderung mit gleichen Chancen an der Hochschulbildung teilhaben können. Hochschulen und Studentenwerke haben in barrierefreie Strukturen investiert, spezielle Beratungsangebote entwickelt und ein System von Nachteilsausgleichen installiert.

Diesen Artikel in Leichte Sprache

Junge Menschen dürfen auf Grund ihrer Behinderung oder chronischen Krankheit vom Studium an der Hochschule ihrer Wahl nicht ausgeschlossen werden. Deshalb haben die Hochschulen als gesellschaftlichen Auftrag dafür Sorge zu tragen, dass behinderte oder chronisch kranke Studierende in ihrem Studium nicht benachteiligt werden und die Angebote der Hochschule möglichst ohne fremde Hilfe in Anspruch nehmen können. Das ist mittlerweile weitgehend im Landesrecht kodifiziert. Damit wurde dem Paradigmenwechsel in der Behindertenpolitik auch auf dem Gebiet der Hochschulbildung Rechnung getragen.

Im Zuge des Bologna-Prozesses und der Föderalismusreform haben sich Studienstruktur, Zulassungsverfahren und Studienbedingungen an deutschen Hochschulen grundlegend geändert. Das bringt dort, wo die Umsetzung gut gelungen ist, überwiegend Vorteile, weil z.B. der erste Abschluss früher erreicht wird, Studierende früher Rückmeldungen durch ihre Professorinnen und Professoren erhalten, mehr und früher individuell beraten wird, das Studienangebot vielfältiger und damit auch für individuelle Bedarfe besser zugeschnitten ist. Unabhängig vom Bologna-Prozess gibt es auch durch die zunehmende Einführung von e-learning-Anteilen im Studium Erleichterungen. An vielen Hochschulen ist aber durch den Wegfall von zeitlichen Gestaltungsspielräumen im Studium, enge organisatorische Vorgaben, eine hohe Prüfungsdichte und hochschuleigene Zulassungsverfahren der Studienablauf für behinderte Studierende und Studienbewerber auch schwieriger geworden. Die Mitgliederversammlung der Hochschulrektorenkonferenz hat sich deshalb mit der am 21. April 2009 in Aachen einstimmig beschlossenen Empfehlung „Eine Hochschule für alle" darauf verständigt, Barrieren zu identifizieren und Maßnahmen zur Herstellung von Chancengerechtigkeit für Studierende mit Behinderung/chronischer Krankheit einzuleiten.

Die Organisation des Studiums und des studentischen Alltags birgt gerade für Studierende mit Behinderung/chronischer Krankheit eine Vielzahl von Herausforderungen. Diese umfassen etwa die Wahl des Studiengangs, der Hochschule und des konkreten Wohnorts, Fragen zur Krankenversicherung, zur Finanzierung des Studiums, zu möglichen Nachteilsausgleichen im Studium oder zur Organisation eines Auslandsstudiums. Unterstützung vor Ort finden Sie dabei bei den Berater/innen und Beauftragten für die Belange der Studierenden mit Behinderung/chronischer Krankheit in Hochschulen und Studentenwerken.

Informationen zum Thema finden Studieninteressierte und Studierende auf den Internetseiten der Informations- und Beratungsstelle Studium und Behinderung (IBS) des Deutschen Studentenwerks (www.studentenwerke.de/behinderung) sowie in der Broschüre "Studium und Behinderung" der Informations- und Beratungsstelle Studium und Behinderung (IBS) des deutschen Studentenwerks.

Studieren mit Behinderung

Behinderte Menschen sollen auch studieren können.
Wie alle anderen Menschen auch.

Deshalb darf es keine Hindernisse
für behinderte Menschen geben.

Die Hoch-Schulen müssen gut für alle Menschen sein.

Zum Beispiel:

- Hoch-Schulen brauchen Aufzüge und Rampen
  für Menschen im Rollstuhl.

Für alle Studentinnen und Studenten mit Behinderungen
muss es gute Beratung über das Studium geben.

Die Studentinnen und Studenten mit Behinderungen
brauchen manchmal besondere Unterstützung.

Zum Beispiel:

- Gehörlose Menschen brauchen einen Gebärden-Dolmetscher.
  Damit sie verstehen können, was der Professor erklärt.

- Blinde Menschen brauchen Bücher oder Papiere in Blindenschrift.
  Oder sie brauchen die Texte auf dem Computer.
  Dann können sie die Texte selber lesen.

Figure 1: Comparison of AS and LS article from `http://www.einfach-teilhaben.de`

("He provides them with advice and information.")

Figure 2 shows the dendrogram of the clustering of the AS texts. A dendrogram shows the results of a hierarchical agglomerative clustering. At the bottom of the dendrogram every paragraph is marked by an individual line. At the points where two vertical paths join, the corresponding clusters are merged to a new larger cluster. The Y-axis is the dissimilarity value of the two clusters. In our experiment the resulting clusters are the clusters at dissimilarity $1 - 1^{-10}$. Geometrically this is a horizontal cut just below dissimilarity 1.0. As can be seen from Figure 2, many of the paragraphs in the left half of the picture are never merged to a slightly larger cluster but are directly connected to the universal cluster that merges everything. This is because they contain only stopwords or only words that do not appear in all paragraphs of another cluster. Such an unbalanced clustering, where many paragraphs are clustered to one cluster and many other paragraphs remain singleton clusters, reduces the precision of the hierarchical approach.

4 Conclusion and Outlook

In this paper we have reported our experiments in creating a monolingual parallel corpus using German/Simple German documents from the web. We have shown that little work has been done on automatic simplification of German so far. We have described our plan to build a statistical machine translation (SMT) system that translates form German into Simple German. SMT systems require parallel corpora. The process of creating a parallel corpus for use in machine translation involves sentence alignment. Sentence alignment algorithms for bilingual corpora differ from those for monolingual corpora. Since all of our data was from the same language, we applied the monolingual sentence alignment approach of Barzilay and Elhadad (2003). We have shown the limits of the algorithm with respect to the language and domain of our data. For example, named entity recognition, a preprocessing step to clustering, is harder for German than for English, the language Barzilay and Elhadad (2003) worked with. Moreover, German features richer morphology than English, which leads to less lexical overlap when working on the word form level.

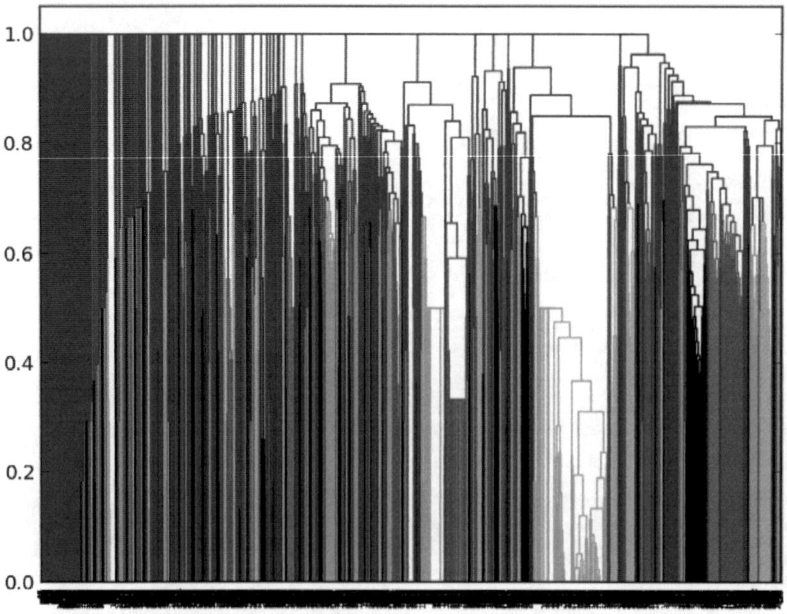

Figure 2: Dendrogram of AS clusters

The domain of our corpus was also broader than that of Barzilay and Elhadad (2003), who used city descriptions from an encyclopedia for their experiments. This made it harder to identify common article structures that could be exploited in clustering.

As a next step, we will experiment with other monolingual sentence alignment algorithms. In addition, we will build a second parallel corpus for German/Simple German: A person familiar with the task of text simplification will produce simple versions of German texts. We will use the resulting parallel corpus as data for our experiments in automatically translating from German to Simple German. The parallel corpus we compiled as part of the work described in this paper can be made available to interested parties upon request.

References

Regina Barzilay and Noemie Elhadad. 2003. Sentence alignment for monolingual comparable corpora. In *Proceedings of EMNLP*.

Stefan Bott and Horacio Saggion. 2011. An unsupervised alignment algorithm for text simplification corpus construction. In *Proceedings of the Workshop on Monolingual Text-To-Text Generation*, MTTG '11, pages 20–26, Stroudsburg, PA, USA.

Stefan Bott, Horacio Saggion, and David Figueroa. 2012. A Hybrid System for Spanish Text Simplification. In *Proceedings of the Third Workshop on Speech and Language Processing for Assistive Technologies*, pages 75–84, Montréal, Canada, June.

Laetitia Brouwers, Delphine Bernhard, Anne-Laure Ligozat, and Thomas François. 2012. Simplification syntaxique de phrases pour le français. In *Actes de la conférence conjointe JEP-TALN-RECITAL 2012, volume 2: TALN*, pages 211–224.

David Chiang. 2005. A Hierarchical Phrase-based Model for Statistical Machine Translation. In *ACL-05: 43rd Annual Meeting of the Association for Computational Linguistics*, pages 263–270, University of Michigan, Ann Arbor, Michigan, USA.

William Coster and David Kauchak. 2011a. Learning to simplify sentences using Wikipedia. In *Proceedings of the Workshop on Monolingual Text-To-Text Generation*, MTTG '11, pages 1–9, Stroudsburg, PA, USA.

William Coster and David Kauchak. 2011b. Simple English Wikipedia: a new text simplification task. In *Proceedings of the 49th Annual Meeting of the Association for Computational Linguistics: Human Language Technologies: short papers - Volume 2*, HLT '11, pages 665–669, Stroudsburg, PA, USA.

George Doddington. 2002. Automatic Evaluation of Machine Translation Quality Using N-gram Co-occurrence Statistics. In *HLT 2002: Human Language Technology Conference, Proceedings of the Second International Conference on Human Language Technology Research*, pages 138–145, San Diego, California.

Caroline Gasperin, Erick Maziero, and Sandra M. Aluisio. 2010. Challenging choices for text simplification. In *Computational Processing of the Portuguese Language. Proceedings of the 9th International Conference, PROPOR 2010*, volume 6001 of *Lecture Notes in Artificial Intelligence (LNAI)*, pages 40–50, Porto Alegre, RS, Brazil. Springer.

A. Gutjahr. 2006. *Lesekompetenz Gehörloser: Ein Forschungsüberblick*. Universität Hamburg.

Hieu Hoang. 2007. Factored Translation Models. In *EMNLP-CoNLL 2007: Proceedings of the 2007 Joint Conference on Empirical Methods in Natural Language Processing and Computational Natural Language Learning*, pages 868–876, Prague, Czech Republic.

Eric Jones, Travis Oliphant, Pearu Peterson, et al. 2001. SciPy: Open Source Scientific Tools for Python.

Philipp Koehn, Hieu Hoang, Alexandra Birch, Chris Callison-Burch, Marcello Federico, Nicola Bertoldi, Brooke Cowan, Wade Shen, Christine Moran, Richard Zens, Chris Dyer, Ondřej Bojar, Alexandra Constantin, and Evan Herbst. 2007. Moses: Open Source Toolkit for Statistical Machine Translation. In *ACL 2007, Proceedings of the 45th Annual Meeting of the Association for Computational Linguistics*, pages 177–180, Prague, Czech Republic.

Kerstin Matausch and Annika Nietzio. 2012. Easy-to-read and plain language: Defining criteria and refining rules. `http://www.w3.org/WAI/RD/2012/easy-to-read/paper11/`.

Rani Nelken and Stuart M. Shieber. 2006. Towards robust context-sensitive sentence alignment for monolingual corpora. In *Proceedings of 11th Conference of the European Chapter of the Association for Computational Linguistics*, pages 161–168.

Kishore Papineni, Salim Roukos, Todd Ward, and Wei-Jing Zhu. 2002. BLEU: a Method for Automatic Evaluation of Machine Translation. In *40th Annual Meeting of the Association for Computational Linguistics, Proceedings of the Conference*, pages 311–318, Philadelphia, PA, USA.

Chris Quirk, Chris Brocket, and William Dolan. 2004. Monolingual machine translation for paraphrase generation. In *Proceedings Empirical Methods in Natural Language Processing*.

Philip Resnik. 1999. Mining the Web for Bilingual Text. In *37th Annual Meeting of the Association for Computational Linguistics, Proceedings of the Conference*, pages 527–534, University of Maryland, College Park, Maryland, USA.

Robert E. Schapire and Yoram Singer. 2000. BoosTexter: A boosting-based system for text categorization. *Machine Learning*, 39(2–3):135–168.

Lucia Specia. 2010. Translating from complex to simplified sentences. In *Computational Processing of the Portuguese Language. Proceedings of the 9th International Conference, PROPOR 2010*, volume 6001 of *Lecture Notes in Artificial Intelligence (LNAI)*, pages 30–39, Porto Alegre, RS, Brazil. Springer.

Sander Wubben, Antal van den Bosch, and Emiel Krahmer. 2012. Sentence simplification by monolingual machine translation. In *Proceedings of the 50th Annual Meeting of the Association for Computational Linguistics: Long Papers - Volume 1*, ACL '12, pages 1015–1024, Jeju Island, Korea.

Mark Yatskar, Bo Pang, Cristian Danescu-Niculescu-Mizil, and Lillian Lee. 2010. For the sake of simplicity: Unsupervised extraction of lexical simplifications from Wikipedia. In *Proceedings of the Annual Meeting of the North American Chapter of the Association for Computational Linguistics*, pages 365–368.

Z. Zhu, D. Bernhard, and I. Gurevych. 2010. A monolingual tree-based translation model for sentence simplification. In *Proceedings of the International Conference on Computational Linguistics*, pages 1353–1361.

The C-Score – Proposing a Reading Comprehension Metrics as a Common Evaluation Measure for Text Simplification

Irina Temnikova
Linguistic Modelling Department,
Institute of Information
and Communication Technologies,
Bulgarian Academy of Sciences
irina.temnikova@gmail.com

Galina Maneva
Lab. of Particle and Astroparticle Physics,
Institute of Nuclear Research
and Nuclear Energy,
Bulgarian Academy of Sciences
galina.maneva@gmail.com

Abstract

This article addresses the lack of common approaches for text simplification evaluation, by presenting the first attempt for a common evaluation metrics. The article proposes reading comprehension evaluation as a method for evaluating the results of Text Simplification (TS). An experiment, as an example application of the evaluation method, as well as three formulae to quantify reading comprehension, are presented. The formulae produce an unique score, the C-score, which gives an estimation of user's reading comprehension of a certain text. The score can be used to evaluate the performance of a text simplification engine on pairs of complex and simplified texts, or to compare the performances of different TS methods using the same texts. The approach can be particularly useful for the modern crowdsourcing approaches, such as those employing the Amazon's Mechanical Turk[1] or CrowdFlower[2]. The aim of this paper is thus to propose an evaluation approach and to motivate the TS community to start a relevant discussion, in order to come up with a common evaluation metrics for this task.

1 Context and Motivation

Currently, the area of Text Simplification (TS) is getting more and more attention. Starting as early as in the 1996, Chandrasekar et al. proposed an approach for TS as a pre-processing step before feeding the text to a parser. Next, the PSET project (Devlin, 1999; Canning, 2002), proposed two modules for simplifying text for aphasic readers. The text simplification approaches continued in 2003 with Siddharthan (2003) and Inui et al. (2003), and through the 2005-2006 until the recent explosion of TS approaches in 2010-2012. Recently, several TS-related workshops took place: PITR 2012 (Williams et al., 2012), SLPAT 2012 (Alexandersson et al., 2012), and NLP4ITA 2012[3] and 2013. As in confirmation with the text simplification definition as the "process for reducing text complexity at different levels" (Temnikova, 2012), the TS approaches tackle a variety of text complexity aspects, ranging from lexical (Devlin, 1999; Inui et al., 2003; Elhadad, 2006; Gasperin et al., 2009; Yatskar et al., 2010; Coster and Kauchak, 2011; Bott et al., 2012; Specia et al., 2012; Rello et al., 2013; Drndarević et al., 2013), syntactic (Chandrasekar et al., 1996; Canning, 2002; Siddharthan, 2003; Inui et al., 2003; Gasperin et al., 2009; Zhu et al., 2010; Woodsend and Lapata, 2011; Coster and Kauchak, 2011; Drndarević et al., 2013), to discourse/cohesion (Siddharthan, 2003). The variety of problems tackled by the TS approaches differ, according to their final aim: (1) being a pre-processing step of an input to text processing applications, or (2) addressing the reading difficulties of specific groups of readers. The first type of final application ranges between parser input (Chandrasekar et al., 1996), small screens displays (Daelemans et al., 2004; Grefenstette, 1998), text summarization (Vanderwende et al., 2007), text extraction (Klebanov et al., 2004), semantic role labeling (Vickrey and Koller, 2008) and Machine Translation (MT) (Ruffino, 1982; Streiff, 1985).The TS approaches addressing specific human reading needs, instead, address readers with low levels of literacy (Siddharthan, 2003;

[1] http://aws.amazon.com/mturk/. Last accessed on May 3rd, 2013.

[2] http://crowdflower.com/. Last accessed on June 14th, 2013.

[3] http://www.taln.upf.edu/nlp4ita/. Last accessed on May 3rd, 2013.

Gasperin et al., 2009; Elhadad, 2006; Williams and Reiter, 2008), language learners (Petersen and Ostendorf, 2007), and readers with specific cognitive and language disabilities. The TS approaches, addressing this last type of readers target those suffering from aphasia (Devlin, 1999; Canning, 2002), deaf readers (Inui et al., 2003), dyslexics (Rello et al., 2013) and the readers with general disabilities (Max, 2006; Drndarević et al., 2013).

Despite the large number of current work in TS, there has been almost no attention to defining common text simplification evaluation approaches, which would allow the comparison of different TS systems. Until the present moment, usually, each approach has applied his/her own methods and materials, often taken from other Natural Language Processing (NLP) fields, making the comparison difficult or impossible.

The aim of this paper is thus to propose an evaluation method and to foster the discussion of this topic in the text simplification community, as well as to motivate the TS community to come up with common evaluation metrics for this task.

Next, Section 2 will describe the existing approaches to evaluating TS, as well as the few attempts towards offering a common evaluation strategy. After that, the next sections will present our evaluation approach, starting with Section 3 describing its context, Section 4 presenting the formulae, Section 5 offering the results, and finally Section 6, providing a Discussion and the Conclusions.

2 Evaluation Methods in Text Simplification

As mentioned in the previous section, until now, the different authors adopted different combinations of metrics, without reaching to a common approach, which would allow the comparison of different systems. As the different TS evaluation methods are applied on a variety of different text units (words, sentences, texts), this makes the comparison between approaches even harder. As the aim of this article is to propose a text simplification evaluation metrics which would take into account text comprehensibility and reading comprehension, in this discussion we will focus mostly on the approaches, whose aim is to simplify texts for target readers and their evaluation strategies.

The existing TS evaluation approaches focus either on the quality of the generated text/sentences, or on the effectiveness of text simplification on reading comprehension. The first group of approaches include human judges ratings of simplification, content preservation, and grammaticality, standard MT evaluation scores (BLEU and NIST), a variety of other automatic metrics (perplexity, precision/recall/F-measure, and edit distance). The methods, aiming to evaluate the text simplification impact on reading comprehension, use, instead, reading speed, reading errors, speech errors, comprehension questions, answer correctness, and users' feedback. Several approaches use a variety of readability formulae (the Flesch, Flesch-Kincaid, Coleman-Liau, and Lorge formulae for English, as well as readability formulae for other languages, such as for Spanish). Due to the criticisms of readability formulae (DuBay, 2004), which often restrict themselves to a very superficial text level, they can be considered to stand on the borderline between the two previously described groups of TS evaluation approaches. As can be seen from the discussion below, different TS systems employ a combination of the listed evaluation approaches.

As one of the first text simplification systems for target reader populations, PSET, seems to have applied different evaluation strategies for different of its components, without running an evaluation of the system as a whole. The lexical simplification component (Devlin, 1999), which replaced technical terms with more frequent synonyms, was evaluated via user feedback, comprehension questions and the use of the Lorge readability formula (Lorge, 1948). The syntactic simplification system evaluated its single components and the system as a whole from different points of view, to a different extent, and used different evaluation strategies. Namely, the text comprehensibility was evaluated via reading time and answers' correctness given by sixteen aphasic readers; the components replacing passive with active voice and splitting sentences were evaluated for content preservation and grammaticality via four human judges' ratings; and finally, the anaphora resolution component was evaluated using precision and recall. Siddharthan (2003) did not carry out evaluation with target readers, while three human judges rated the grammaticality and the meaning preservation of ninety-five sentences. Gasperin et al. (2009) used precision, recall and f-measure. Other approaches, using human judges are those of Elhadad (2006), who also used precision and recall and Yatskar et al. (2010), who employed three annotators comparing pairs of words and indicating them same, simpler, or more complex. Williams and Reiter (2008) run two experiments, the larger one involving 230 subjects and measured oral reading rate, oral reading errors, response correctness to comprehension questions and finally, speech errors. Drndarevic et al. (2013) used 7 readability measures for Spanish to evaluate the degree of simplification, and twenty-five human annotators to evaluate on a Likert scale the grammaticality of the output and the preservation of the original meaning. The recent approaches considering TS as an MT task, such as Specia (2010), Zhu et al. (2010), Coster and Kauchak (2011) and Woodsend and Lapata (2011), apply standard MT evaluation techniques, such as BLEU (Papineni et al., 2002), NIST (Doddington, 2002), and TERp (Snover et al., 2009). In addition, Woodsend and Lapata (2011) apply two readability measures (Flesch-Kincaid, Coleman-Liau) to evaluate the actual reduction in complexity and human judges ratings for simplification, meaning preservation, and grammaticality. Zhu et al. (2010) apply the Flesch readability score (Flesch, 1948) and n-gram language model perplexity, and Coster and Kauchak (2011) – two additional automatic techniques (the word-level-F1 and simple string accuracy), taken from sentence compression evaluation (Clarke and Lapata, 2006).

As we consider that the aim of text simplification for human readers is to improve text comprehensibility, we argue that reading comprehension must be evaluated, and that evaluating just the quality of produced sentences is not enough. Differently from the approaches that employ human judges, we consider that it is better to test real human comprehension with target readers populations, rather than to make conclusions about the extent of population's understanding on the basis of the opinion of a small number of human judges. In addition, we consider that measuring reading speed, rate, as well as reading and speed errors, requires much more complicated and expensive tools, than having an online system to measure time to reply and recognize correct answers. Finally, we consider that cloze tests are an evaluation method that cannot really reflect the complexity of reading comprehension (for example for measuring manipulations of the syntactic structure of sentences), and for this reason, we select multiple-choice questions as the testing method, which we consider the most reflecting the specificities of the complexity of a text, more accessible than eye-tracking technologies, and more objective than users' feedback. The approach does not explicitly evaluate the fluency, grammaticality and content preservation of the simplified text, but can be coupled with such additional evaluation.

The closest to ours approach is that of Rello et al. (2013) who evaluated reading comprehension with over ninety readers with and without dyslexia. Besides using eye-tracking (reading time and fixations duration), different reading devices, and users rating the text according to how easy it is it read, to understand and to remember, they obtain also a comprehension score based on multiple-choice questions (MCQ) with 3 answers (1 correct, 1 partially correct and 1 wrong). The difference with our approach is that we consider that having only one correct answer (as suggested by Gronlund (1982)), is a more objective evaluation, rather than having one partially correct answer, which would introduce subjectivity in evaluation.

To support our motivation, some state-of-the-art approaches state the scarcity of evaluation with target readers (Williams and Reiter, 2008), note that there are no commonly accepted evaluation measures (Coster and Kauchak, 2011), attempt to address the need of developing reading comprehension evaluation methods (Siddharthan and Katsos, 2012), and propose common evaluation frameworks (Specia et al., 2012; De Belder and Moens, 2012). More concretely, Siddhathan and Katsos (2012) propose the magnitude estimation of readability judgements and the delayed sentence recall as reading comprehension evaluation methods. Specia et al. (2012) provide a lexical simplification evaluation framework in the context of Semeval-2012. The evaluation is performed using a measure of inter-annotator agreement, based on Cohen (1960). Similarly, De Belder and Moens (2012) propose a dataset for evaluating lexical simplification. No common evaluation framework has been yet developed for syntactic simplification.

As seen in the overview, besides the multitude of existing approaches, and the few approaches attempting to propose a common evaluation framework, there are no widely accepted evaluation metrics or methods, which would allow the comparison of existing approaches. The next section presents our evaluation approach, which we offer as a candidate for common evaluation metrics.

3 Proposed Evaluation Metrics

3.1 The Evaluation Experiment

The metrics proposed in this article, was developed in the context of a previously conducted large-scale text simplification evaluation experiment (Temnikova, 2012). The experiment aimed to determine whether a manual, rule-based text simplification approach (namely a controlled language), can re-write existing texts into more understandable versions. Impact on reading comprehension was necessary to evaluate, as the purpose of text simplification was to enhance in first place the reading comprehension of emergency instructions. The controlled language used for simplification was the Controlled Language for Crisis Management (CLCM, more details in (Temnikova, 2012)), which was developed on the basis of existing psychological and psycholinguistic literature discussing human comprehension under stress, which ensures its psychological validity. The text units evaluated in this experiments were whole texts, and more concretely pairs of original texts and their simplified versions. We argue that using whole texts for measuring reading comprehension is better than single sentences, as the texts provide more context for understanding. The experiment took place in the format of an online experiment, conducted via a specially developed web interface, and required users to read several texts and answer Multiple-Choice Questions (MCQ), testing the readers' understanding of each of the texts. Due to the purpose of the text simplification (emergency situations simulation), users were required to read the texts in a limited time, as to imitate a stressful situation with no time to think and re-read the text. This aspect will not be taken into account in the evaluation, as the purpose is to propose a general formula, applicable to a variety of different text simplification experiments. After reading the text in a limited time, the text was hidden from the readers, and they were presented with a screen, asking if they were ready to proceed with the questions. Next, each question was displayed one by one, along with its answers, with the readers not having the option to go back to the text. In order to ensure the constant attention of the readers and to reduce readers' tiredness fact or, the texts were kept short (about 150-170 words each), and the number of texts to be read by the reader was kept to four. In addition, to ensure comparability, all the texts were selected in a way to be more or less of the same length. The experiment employed a collection of a total of eight texts, four of which original, non simplified ('complex') versions, and the other four – their manually simplified versions. Each user had to read two complex and two simplified texts, none of which was a variant of the other. The interface automatically randomized the order of displaying the texts, to ensure that different users would get different combinations of texts in one of the following two different sequences:

- Complex-Simplified-Complex-Simplified
- Simplified-Complex-Simplified-Complex

This was done in order to minimize the impact of the order of displaying the texts on the text comprehension results. After reading each text, the readers were prompted to answer between four and five questions about each text. The MCQ method was selected as it is considered being the most objective and easily measurable way of assessing comprehension (Gronlund, 1982). The number of questions and answers was selected in a way to not tire the reader (four to five questions per text and four to five answers for each question), and the questions and answers themselves were designed following the the best MCQ practices (Gronlund, 1982). Some of the practices followed involved ensuring that there is only one correct answer per question, making all wrong answers (or 'distractors') grammatically, and as text length consistent with the correct answer, in order to avoid giving hints to the reader, and making all distractors plausible and equally attractive. Similarly to the texts, the questions and answers were also displayed in different order to different readers, to avoid that the order influences the comprehension results. The correct answer was displayed in different positions to avoid learning its position and internally marked in a way to distinguish it during evaluation from all the distractors in whatever position it was displayed. The questions required understanding of key aspects of the texts, to avoid relying on pure texts' memorization (such as under which conditions what was supposed to be done, explanations, and the order in which actions needed to be taken). The information, evaluating the users' comprehension, collected during the experiment, was, on one hand the time for answering each question, and on the other hand, the number of correct answers given by all participants while replying to the same question. Besides the fact that we used a specially developed interface, this evaluation approach can be applied to any experiment employing an interface capable of calculating the time for answering and to distinguish the correct answers from the incorrect ones.

The efficiency of the experiment design was thoroughly tested by running it through several rounds of pilot experiments and requiring participants' feedback.

We claim that the evaluation approach proposed in this paper can be applied to more simply organized experiments, as the randomization aspects are not reflected in the evaluation formulae.

The final experiment involved 103 participants, collected via a request sent to several mailing lists. The participants were 55 percent women and 44 percent male, and ranged from undergraduate students to retired academicians (i.e. corresponded to nineteen to fifty-nine years old). As the experiment allowed entering lots of personal data, it was also known that participants had a variety of professions (including NLP people, teachers, and lawyers), knew English from the beginner through intermediate, to native level, and spoke a large variety of native languages, allowing to have native speakers from many of the World's language families (Non Indo-European and Indo-European included). Figure 1 shows the coarse-grained classification made at the time of the experiment, and the distribution of participants per native languages. A subset of specific native language participants will be selected to give an example of applying the evaluation metrics to a real evaluation experiment.

In order to obtain results, we have asked the participants to enter a rich selection of information, and recorded the chosen answer (be it correct or not), and the time which each participant employed to give each answer (correct or wrong). Table 1 shows the data we recorded for each single answer of every participant.

The data in Table 1 is: *Entry id* is each given answer, the *Domain background* (answer *y* – yes and *n* – no) indicates whether the participant has any previous knowledge of the experiment (crisis management) domain. As each text, question and com-

Type	**Example**
Entry id	1
Age of the participant	24
Gender of the participant	f
Profession of the participant	Student
Domain background (y/n)	n
Native lang.	English
Level of English	Native
Text number	4
Exper. completed (0/1)	1
User number	1
Question number	30
Answer number	0
Time to reply	18695
Texts pair number	1

Table 1: Participant's information recorded for each answer.

plex/simplified texts pair are given reference numbers, respectively *Text number*, *Question number*, and *Texts pair number* record that. As required by the evaluation method, each entry records also the *Time to reply* each question (measured in 'milliseconds'), and the *Answer number*. As said before, the correct answers are marked in a special way, allowing to distinguish them at a later stage, when counting the number of correct answers.

3.2 Definitions and Evaluation Hypotheses

In order to correctly evaluate the performance of the text simplification method on the basis of the above described experiment, the data obtained was thoughtfully analyzed. The two criteria selected to best describe the users' performance were time to reply and number of correct answers. The evaluation was done offline, after collecting the data from the participants. The evaluation analysis aimed to test the following **two hypotheses**:

If the text simplification approach has a positive impact on the reading comprehension:

1. The percentage of correct answers given for the simplified text will be higher than the percentage of correct answers given for the complex text.

2. The time to recognize the correct answer and reply correctly to the questions about the simplified text will be significantly lower than the time to recognize the correct answer and

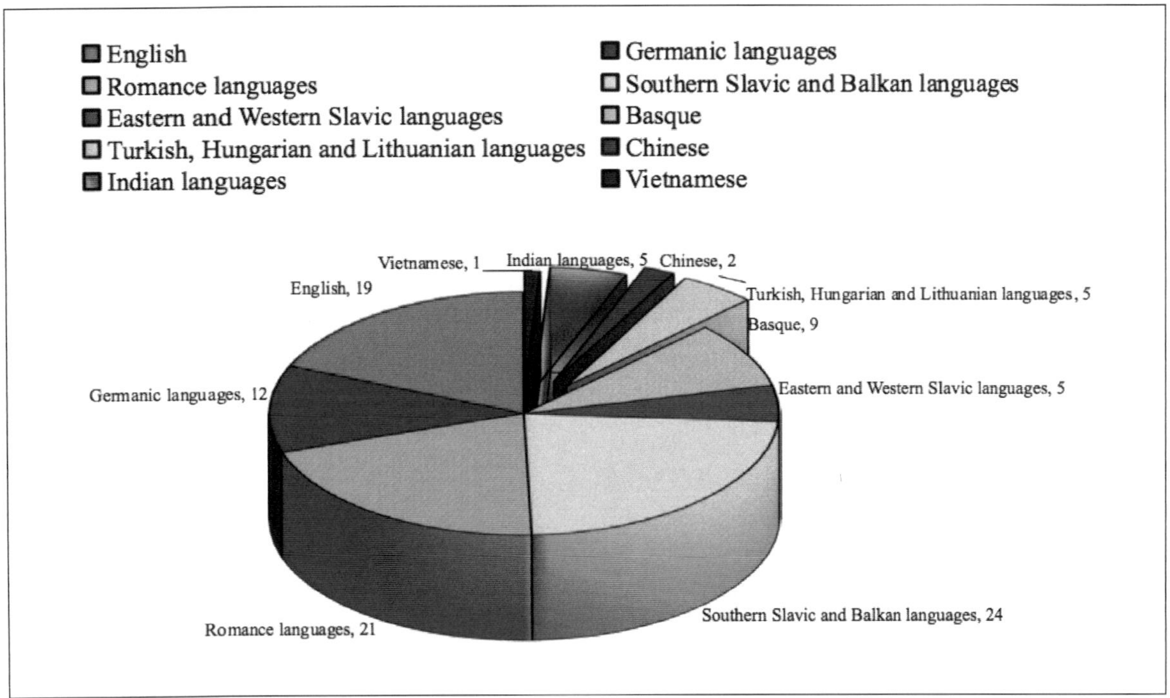

Figure 1: Coarse-grained distribution of participants per native languages.

reply correctly to the questions about the complex text.

The two hypotheses were tested previously by employing only the key variables (time to reply and number of correct answers). It has been proven that comprehension increases with the percentage of correct answers and decreases with the increase of the time to reply. On the basis of these facts, we define the **C-Score** (a text Comprehension Score) – an objective evaluation metrics, which allows to give a reading comprehension estimate to a text, or to compare two texts or two or more text simplification approaches. The C-Score is calculated text per text. In order to address a variety of situations, we propose three versions of the C-Score, which cover, gradually, all possible variables which can affect comprehension in such an experiment. In the following sections we present their formulae, the variables involved, and discuss their results, advantages and shortcomings.

3.3 The C-Score Version One. The C-Score Simple.

Given a text comprehension experiment featuring n texts with m questions with r answers each, an ability to measure time to reply to questions and to recognize the correct answers, we define the *C-Score Simple* as given below:

$$C_{simple} = \frac{Pr}{t_{mean}} \quad (1)$$

Where: *Pr* is the percentage of correct answers, from all answers given to all the questions about this text, and *t* is the average time to reply to all questions about this text (both with a correct and a wrong answer). The time is expressed in arbitrary seconds-based units, depending on the experiment. The logic behind this formula is simple: we consider that comprehension increases with the percentage of correctly answered questions, and diminishes if the mean time to answer questions increases.

3.4 The C-Score Version Two. C-Score Complete.

The C-Score complete takes into consideration a rich selection of variables reflecting the questions and answers complexity. In this C-Score version, we consider that the experiment designers will select short texts (e.g. 150 words) of a similar length, with the aim to reduce participants' tiredness factor, as we did in our experimental settings.

$$C_{complete} = \frac{Pr}{Nq} \sum_{q=1}^{Nq} \frac{Qs(q)}{t_{mean}(q)} \quad (2)$$

In this formula, *Pr* is the percentage of correct answers by all participants for this text, *Nq* is the number of questions of this text (4-5 in our experiment), and *t* is the average time to reply to all questions about this text (4-5 in our experiment). We introduce the concept Question Size, (*Qs*), which is calculated for each question and takes into account the number of answers of the question (*Na*), the question length in words (*Lq*), and the total length in words of its answers (*La*):

$$Qs = Na(Lq + La) \tag{3}$$

We consider that the number of questions negatively influences the comprehension results, as the reader gets cognitively tired to process more and more questions about different key aspects of the text. In addition, Gronlund (1982) suggests to restrict the number of questions per text to four-five to achieve better learning. For this reason, we consider that comprehension decreases, if the number of questions is higher. We also consider that answering correctly/faster to a difficult question shows better text comprehension than giving fast a correct answer to a simply-worded question. For this reason we award question difficulty, and we place it above the fraction.

3.5 The C-Score Version Three. C-Score Textsize.

Finally, the last version of C-Score takes into account the case when the texts used for comparison can be of a different length, and in this way, the texts' complexity (for example, when comparing the results of two different TS engines, without having access to the same texts). For this reason, the C-Score 3 considers the text length (called *text size, Ts*) of the texts used in the experiment. As a longer text will be more difficult to understand than a shorter text, the text length is placed near the *percentage of correct answers*.

$$C_{textsize} = \frac{PrTs}{Nq} \sum_{q=1}^{Nq} \frac{Qs(q)}{t_{mean}(q)} \tag{4}$$

4 C-Score Results

We have implemented and applied the above described formulae to the experimental data, presented in Section 3.1. As we have only one text simplification approach, two user scenarios are presented:

1. Original ('Complex') vs. Simplified ('Simple') pairs of texts comparison. The subset of participants are the speakers of Basque, Turkish, Hungarian, Lithuanian, Vietnamese, Chinese, and Indian languages. All three formulae have been applied.

2. Comparison of the comprehension of the same text of readers from different subgroups. The readers have been divided by age. This scenario can be used to infer psycho-linguistic findings about the reading abilities of different participants.

Please note that the texts pairs are: Text 1 and 2; Text 3 and 4; Text 5 and 6; and Text 7 and 8. In each couple, the first text is complex and the second is its simplified version. The results for the first evaluation scenario are respectively displayed in Table 2 for *C-Score Simple*, Table 3 for *C-Score Complete* and Table 4 for *C-Score Textsize*. The results of C-Score Complete have been multiplied per 100 for better readability. As a reminder, we consider that higher the score is, better is text comprehension. From this point of view, if the text simplification approach was successful, Text 2 (Simplified) should have a higher C-Score than its original, complex Text 1, Text 4 (Simplified) should have a higher C-Score than its original Text 3, Text 6 (Simplified) – a higher score than the complex Text 5, and Text 8 (Simplified) – a higher score than its original Text 7.

In the second scenario, the participants data has been divided into data relevant to participants under 45 years old (ninety-two participants) and into participants over 45 years old (eleven participants). In this case only the C-Score Simple has been applied. The results of this evaluation are shown in Table 5. As our aim is to compare the reading abilities of different ages of people, and not the results of text simplification, only the complex texts are taken into account. The results show that the comprehension score of participants under 45 years old is higher for all texts (despite the uneven participants' distribution), except in the case of complex Text 5.

A similar phenomenon can be observed in Tables 2, 3 and 4, where in all text pairs, except for pair 3, i.e. Texts 5 and 6 (where can be observed the opposite), the simplified text has a higher comprehension score than its complex original. The hypothesis about the different behavior of Text 5 and 6 is that it is text-specific. This is confirmed by Table 5, which shows that besides the big dif-

Text number	C-Score Simple
Text 1 (Complex)	21.3
Text 2 (Simplified)	35.3
Text 3 (Complex)	24.8
Text 4 (Simplified)	34.9
Text 5 (Complex)	36.8
Text 6 (Simplified)	23.6
Text 7 (Complex)	40.5
Text 8 (Simplified)	51.5

Table 2: Experiment results for C-Score Simple.

ferences in reading comprehension between participants under 45 years old and participants over 45 years old, Text 5 has more or less the same comprehension score for both groups of readers. From this fact we can assume that this text is probably fairly easy, so this type of combination of text simplification rules does not simplify it, and instead, when applied makes it less comprehensible or more awkward for the human readers.

Text number	C-Score Complete
Text 1 (Complex)	66.3
Text 2 (Simplified)	114.3
Text 3 (Complex)	65.3
Text 4 (Simplified)	89.9
Text 5 (Complex)	104.0
Text 6 (Simplified)	66.9
Text 7 (Complex)	106.7
Text 8 (Simplified)	153.0

Table 3: Experiment results for C-Score Complete.

Text number	C-Score Textsize
Text 1 (Complex)	109.5
Text 2 (Simplified)	192.0
Text 3 (Complex)	107.7
Text 4 (Simplified)	131.3
Text 5 (Complex)	171.6
Text 6 (Simplified)	102.4
Text 7 (Complex)	176.1
Text 8 (Simplified)	263.3

Table 4: Experiment results for C-ScoreTextsize.

5 Discussion and Conclusions

This article has presented an extended discussion of the methods employed for evaluation in the text simplification domain. In order to address the lack of common or standard evaluation approaches, this article proposed three evaluation formulae, which measure the reading comprehension of produced texts. The formulae have been developed on the basis of an extensive reading comprehension experiment, aiming to evaluate the impact of a text simplification approach (a controlled language) on emergency instructions. Two evaluation scenarios have been presented, the first of which calculated with all three formulae, while the second used only the simplest one. In this way, the article aims to address both the lack of common TS evaluation metrics as suggested in Section 2 (Coster and Kauchak, 2011) and the scarcity of reading comprehension (Siddharthan and Katsos, 2012) evaluation with real users (Williams and Reiter, 2008), by proposing a tailored approach for this type of text simplification evaluation. With this article we aim at inciting the Text Simplification Community to open a discussion forum about common methods for evaluating text simplification, in order to provide objective evaluation metrics allowing the comparison of different approaches, and to ensure that simplification really achieves its aims. We also argue that taking in consideration the end-users and text units used for evaluation is important. In our approach, we address only the evaluation of text simplification approaches aiming to improve reading comprehension and experiments in which time to reply to questions and percentage of correct answers can be measured. A plausible scenario for applying our evaluation approach would be to use the Amazon Mechanical Turk for crowd-sourcing and then to evaluate the performance of a text simplification system on complex and simplified texts, to compare the performance of two or more approaches, or of two versions of the same system on the same pairs of texts. These formulae can be also employed in psycholinguistically-oriented experiments, which aim to reach cognitive findings regarding specific target reader groups, such as dyslexics or autis-

Text number	Under 45	Over 45
Text 1 (Complex)	39.7	22.5
Text 3 (Complex)	37.2	18.4
Text 5 (Complex)	38.4	38.9
Text 7 (Complex)	54.3	35.9

Table 5: C-Score Simple for one text.

tic readers. Future work will involve the comparison of the above proposed evaluation metrics with any of the metrics already employed in the related work, such as the recent and classic readability formulae, eye-tracking, reading rate, human judges ratings, and others. We consider that content preservation and grammaticality are not necessary to be evaluated for this approach, as the simplified texts have been produced manually, by linguists, who were native speakers of English.

Acknowledgments

The authors would like to thank Prof. Dr. Petar Temnikov for the ideas and advices about the research methodology, Dr. Anke Buttner for the psycholinguistic counseling about the experiment design, including questions, answers and texts selection and the simplification method psychological validity, and Dr. Constantin Orasan and Dr. Le An Ha for the testing interface implementation. The research of Irina Temnikova reported in this paper was partially supported by the project AComIn "Advanced Computing for Innovation", grant 316087, funded by the FP7 Capacity Programme (Research Potential of Convergence Regions).

Finally, the authors would also like to thank the PITR 2013 reviewers for their useful feedback.

References

Jan Alexandersson, Peter Ljunglf, Kathleen F. McCoy, Brian Roark, and Annalu Waller, editors. 2012. *Proceedings of the Third Workshop on Speech and Language Processing for Assistive Technologies*. Association for Computational Linguistics, Montréal, Canada, June.

Stefan Bott, Luz Rello, Biljana Drndarević, and Horacio Saggion. 2012. Can spanish be simpler? lexsis: Lexical simplification for spanish. In *Proceedings of the 24th International Conference on Computational Linguistics (Coling 2012), Mumbai, India (December 2012)*.

Yvonne Canning. 2002. *Syntactic Simplification of Text*. Ph.D. thesis, University of Sunderland, UK.

Raman Chandrasekar, Christine Doran, and Bangalore Srinivas. 1996. Motivations and methods for text simplification. In *Proceedings of the 16th conference on Computational linguistics-Volume 2*, pages 1041–1044. Association for Computational Linguistics.

James Clarke and Mirella Lapata. 2006. Models for sentence compression: A comparison across domains, training requirements and evaluation measures. In *Proceedings of the 21st International Conference on Computational Linguistics and the 44th annual meeting of the Association for Computational Linguistics*, pages 377–384. Association for Computational Linguistics.

Jacob Cohen et al. 1960. A coefficient of agreement for nominal scales. *Educational and psychological measurement*, 20(1):37–46.

William Coster and David Kauchak. 2011. Learning to simplify sentences using wikipedia. In *Proceedings of the Workshop on Monolingual Text-To-Text Generation*, pages 1–9. Association for Computational Linguistics.

Walter Daelemans, Anja Höthker, and Erik Tjong Kim Sang. 2004. Automatic sentence simplification for subtitling in dutch and english. In *Proceedings of the 4th International Conference on Language Resources and Evaluation*, pages 1045–1048.

Jan De Belder and Marie-Francine Moens. 2012. A dataset for the evaluation of lexical simplification. In *Computational Linguistics and Intelligent Text Processing*, pages 426–437. Springer.

Siobhan Devlin. 1999. *Automatic Language Simplification for Aphasic Readers*. Ph.D. thesis, University of Sunderland, UK.

George Doddington. 2002. Automatic evaluation of machine translation quality using n-gram co-occurrence statistics. In *Proceedings of the second international conference on Human Language Technology Research*, pages 138–145. Morgan Kaufmann Publishers Inc.

Biljana Drndarević, Sanja Štajner, Stefan Bott, Susana Bautista, and Horacio Saggion. 2013. Automatic text simplification in spanish: A comparative evaluation of complementing modules. In *Computational Linguistics and Intelligent Text Processing*, pages 488–500. Springer.

William H. DuBay. 2004. The principles of readability. *Impact Information*, pages 1–76.

Noémie Elhadad. 2006. *User-sensitive text summarization: Application to the medical domain*. Ph.D. thesis, Columbia University.

Rudolf Flesch. 1948. A new readability yardstick. *The Journal of applied psychology*, 32(3).

Caroline Gasperin, Erick Maziero, Lucia Specia, TAS Pardo, and Sandra M Aluisio. 2009. Natural language processing for social inclusion: a text simplification architecture for different literacy levels. *the Proceedings of SEMISH-XXXVI Seminário Integrado de Software e Hardware*, pages 387–401.

Gregory Grefenstette. 1998. Producing intelligent telegraphic text reduction to provide an audio scanning service for the blind. In *Working notes of the*

AAAI Spring Symposium on Intelligent Text summarization, pages 111–118.

Norman Edward Gronlund. 1982. *Constructing achievement tests*. Prentice Hall.

Kentaro Inui, Atsushi Fujita, Tetsuro Takahashi, Ryu Iida, and Tomoya Iwakura. 2003. Text simplification for reading assistance: a project note. In *Proceedings of the second international workshop on Paraphrasing-Volume 16*, pages 9–16. Association for Computational Linguistics.

Beata Beigman Klebanov, Kevin Knight, and Daniel Marcu. 2004. Text simplification for information-seeking applications. In *On the Move to Meaningful Internet Systems 2004: CoopIS, DOA, and ODBASE*, pages 735–747. Springer.

Irving Lorge. 1948. The lorge and flesch readability formulae: A correction. *School and Society*, 67:141–142.

Aurélien Max. 2006. Writing for language-impaired readers. In *Computational Linguistics and Intelligent Text Processing*, pages 567–570. Springer.

Kishore Papineni, Salim Roukos, Todd Ward, and Wei-Jing Zhu. 2002. Bleu: a method for automatic evaluation of machine translation. In *Proceedings of the 40th annual meeting on association for computational linguistics*, pages 311–318. Association for Computational Linguistics.

Sarah E. Petersen and Mari Ostendorf. 2007. Text simplification for language learners: a corpus analysis. In *In Proc. of Workshop on Speech and Language Technology for Education*.

Luz Rello, Ricardo Baeza-Yates, Stefan Bott, and Horacio Saggion. 2013. Simplify or help? text simplification strategies for people with dyslexia. *Proc. W4A*, 13.

J. Richard Ruffino. 1982. Coping with machine translation. *Practical Experience of Machine Translation*.

Advaith Siddharthan and Napoleon Katsos. 2012. Offline sentence processing measures for testing readability with users. In *Proceedings of the First Workshop on Predicting and Improving Text Readability for target reader populations*, pages 17–24. Association for Computational Linguistics.

Advaith Siddharthan. 2003. *Syntactic simplification and text cohesion*. Ph.D. thesis, University of Cambridge, UK.

Matthew Snover, Nitin Madnani, Bonnie J Dorr, and Richard Schwartz. 2009. Fluency, adequacy, or hter?: exploring different human judgments with a tunable mt metric. In *Proceedings of the Fourth Workshop on Statistical Machine Translation*, pages 259–268. Association for Computational Linguistics.

Lucia Specia, Sujay Kumar Jauhar, and Rada Mihalcea. 2012. Semeval-2012 task 1: English lexical simplification. In *Proceedings of the First Joint Conference on Lexical and Computational Semantics*, pages 347–355. Association for Computational Linguistics.

Lucia Specia. 2010. Translating from complex to simplified sentences. In *Computational Processing of the Portuguese Language*, pages 30–39. Springer.

A. A. Streiff. 1985. New developments in titus 4. *Lawson (1985)*, 185:192.

Irina Temnikova. 2012. *Text Complexity and Text Simplification in the Crisis Management domain*. Ph.D. thesis, Wolverhampton, UK.

Lucy Vanderwende, Hisami Suzuki, Chris Brockett, and Ani Nenkova. 2007. Beyond sumbasic: Task-focused summarization with sentence simplification and lexical expansion. *Information Processing & Management*, 43(6):1606–1618.

David Vickrey and Daphne Koller. 2008. Sentence simplification for semantic role labeling. In *Proceedings of the 46th Annual Meeting of the Association for Computational Linguistics: Human Language Technologies (ACL-2008: HLT)*, pages 344–352.

Sandra Williams and Ehud Reiter. 2008. Generating basic skills reports for low-skilled readers. *Natural Language Engineering*, 14(4):495–525.

Sandra Williams, Advaith Siddharthan, and Ani Nenkova, editors. 2012. *Proceedings of the First Workshop on Predicting and Improving Text Readability for target reader populations*. Association for Computational Linguistics, Montréal, Canada, June.

Kristian Woodsend and Mirella Lapata. 2011. Learning to simplify sentences with quasi-synchronous grammar and integer programming. In *Proceedings of the Conference on Empirical Methods in Natural Language Processing*, pages 409–420. Association for Computational Linguistics.

Mark Yatskar, Bo Pang, Cristian Danescu-Niculescu-Mizil, and Lillian Lee. 2010. For the sake of simplicity: Unsupervised extraction of lexical simplifications from wikipedia. In *Human Language Technologies: The 2010 Annual Conference of the North American Chapter of the Association for Computational Linguistics*, pages 365–368. Association for Computational Linguistics.

Zhemin Zhu, Delphine Bernhard, and Iryna Gurevych. 2010. A monolingual tree-based translation model for sentence simplification. In *Proceedings of the 23rd international conference on computational linguistics*, pages 1353–1361. Association for Computational Linguistics.

A Language-Independent Approach to Automatic Text Difficulty Assessment for Second-Language Learners

Wade Shen[1], Jennifer Williams[1], Tamas Marius[2], and Elizabeth Salesky [†1]

[1]MIT Lincoln Laboratory Human Language Technology Group,
244 Wood Street Lexingon, MA 02420, USA
{swade,jennifer.williams,elizabeth.salesky}@ll.mit.edu

[2]DLI Foreign Language Center, Bldg. 420, Room 119 Monterey, CA 93944, USA
tamas.g.marius.civ@mail.mil

Abstract

In this paper, we introduce a new baseline for language-independent text difficulty assessment applied to the Interagency Language Roundtable (ILR) proficiency scale. We demonstrate that reading level assessment is a discriminative problem that is best-suited for regression. Our baseline uses z-normalized shallow length features and TF-LOG weighted vectors on bag-of-words for Arabic, Dari, English, and Pashto. We compare Support Vector Machines and the Margin-Infused Relaxed Algorithm measured by mean squared error. We provide an analysis of which features are most predictive of a given level.

1 Introduction

The ability to obtain new materials of an appropriate language proficiency level is an obstacle for second-language learners and educators alike. With the growth of publicly available Internet and news sources, learners and instructors of foreign languages should have ever-increasing access to large volumes of foreign language text. However, sifting through this pool of foreign language data poses a significant challenge. In this paper we demonstrate two machine learning regression methods which can be used to help both learners and course developers by automatically rating documents based on the text difficulty. These methods can be used to automatically identify documents at specific levels in order to speed course or test development, providing learners with custom-tailored materials that match their learning needs.

ILR (Interagency Language Roundtable) levels reflect differences in text difficulty for second-language learners at different stages of their education. A description of each level is shown in Table 1 (Interagency Language Roundtable, 2013). Some levels differ in terms of sentence structure, length of document, type of communication, etc., while others, especially the higher levels, differ in terms of the domain and style of writing. Given these differences, we expect that both semantic content and grammar-related features will be necessary to distinguish between documents at different levels.

Level	Description
0	No proficiency
0+	Memorized proficiency
1	Elementary proficiency
1+	Elementary proficiency, plus
2	Limited working proficiency
2+	Limited working proficiency, plus
3	General professional proficiency
3+	General professional proficiency, plus
4	Advanced professional proficienty
4+	Advanced professional proficiency, plus
5	Functionally native proficiency

Table 1: Description of ILR levels.

Automatically determining ILR levels from documents is a research problem without known solutions. We have developed and adapted a series of rating algorithms and a set of experiments gauging the feasibility of automatic ILR level assignment for text documents. Using data provided by the Defense Language Institute Foreign Language Center (DLIFLC), we show that while the problem is tractable, the performance of automatic

[†] This work was sponsored by the Department of Defense under Air Force Contract FA8721-05-C-0002. Opinions, interpretations, conclusions, and recommendations are those of the authors and are not necessarily endorsed by the United States Government.

methods is not perfect.

Our general approach treats the ILR rating problem as one of text classification; given the contents and structure of a document, which of the ILR levels should this document be assigned to? This differs from traditional topic classification tasks where word-usage often uniquely defines topics, since we are also interested in features of text complexity that describe structure. Leveling text is a problem better fit to regression because reading level is a continuous scale. We want to know how close a document is to a given level (or between levels), so we measured performance using mean squared error (MSE). We show that language-independent features can be used for regression with Support Vector Machines (SVMs) and the Margin-Infused Relaxed Algorithm (MIRA), and we present our results for this new baseline for Arabic, Dari, English, and Pashto. To the best of our knowledge, this is the first study to systematically examine a language-independent approach to readability using the ILR rating scale for second-language learners.

This paper is structured as follows: Section 2 describes previous work on reading level assessment as a text classification problem, Section 3 describes the two algorithms that we used in our present work, Section 4 describes our data and experiments, Section 5 reports our results, Section 6 provides an analysis of our results, and Section 7 proposes different kinds of future work that can be done to improve this baseline.

2 Related Work

In this section we describe some work on the readability problem that is most closely related to our own.

One of the earliest formulas for reading level assessment, called the Flesch Reading Ease Formula, measured readability based on shallow length features (Flesch, 1948). This metric included two measurements: the average number of words per sentence and the average number of syllables per word. Although these features appear to be shallow at the offset, the number of syllables per word could be taken as an abstraction of word complexity. Those formulas, as well as their various revisions, have become popular because they are easy to compute for a variety of applications, including structuring highly technical text that is comprehensible at lower reading levels (Kincaid et al., 1975). Some of the revisions to the Flesch Reading Ease Formula have included weighting these shallow features in order to linearly regress across different difficulty levels.

Much effort has been placed into automating the scoring process, and recent work on this issue has examined machine learning methods to treat reading level as a text classification problem. Schwarm and Ostendorf (2005) worked on automatically classifying text by grade level for first-language learners. Their machine learning approach was a one vs. all method using a set of SVM binary classifiers that were constructed for each grade level category: 2, 3, 4, and 5. The following features were used for classfication: average sentence length, average number of syllables per word, Flesch-Kincaid score, 6 out-of-vocabulary (OOV) rate scores, syntactic parse features, and 12 language model perplexity scores. Their data was taken from the Weekly Reader newspaper, already separated by grade level. They found that the error rate for misclassification by more than one grade level was significantly lower for the SVM classifier than for both Lexile and Flesch-Kincaid. Petersen and Ostendorf (2009) later replicated and expanded Schwarm and Ostendorf (2005), reaffirming that both classification and regression with SVMs provided a better approximation of readabilty by grade level when compared with more traditional methods such as the Flesch-Kincaid score. In the current work, we also use SVM for regression, but have decided to report mean squared error as a more meaningful metric.

In an effort to uncover which features are the most salient for discriminating among reading levels, Feng et al., (2010) studied classification performance using combinations of different kinds of readability features using data from the Weekly Reader newspaper. Their work examined the following types of features: discourse, language modeling, parsed syntactic features, POS features, shallow length features, as well as some features replicated from Schwarm and Ostendorf (2005). They reported classifier accuracy and mean squared error from two classifiers, SVM and Logistic Regression, which were used to predict grade level for grades 2 through 5. While they found that POS features were the most predictive overall, they also found that the average number of words per sentence was the most predictive length feature. This length feature alone achieved 52% accuracy with the Logistic Regression classifier. In the present work, we use the average number of words per sentence as a length feature and show that this metric has some correspondence with the different ILR levels.

Another way to examine readability is to treat it as a sorting problem; that is, given some collection of texts, to sort them from easiest to most difficult. Tanaka-Ishii et al., (2010) presented a novel method for determining readibility based on sorting texts using text from two groups: low difficulty and high difficulty. They reported their results in terms of the Spearman correlation coefficient to compare performance of Flesch-Kincaid, Dale-Chall, SVM regression, and their sorting method. They showed that their sorting method was superior to the other methods, followed by SVM regression. However, they call for a more modern and efficient approach to the problem, such as online learning, that would estimate weights for regression. We answer their call with an online learning approach in this work.

3 Algorithms

In this section, we describe two maximum margin approaches that we used in our experiments. Both are based on the principle of structural risk minimization. We selected the SVM algorithm because of its proven usefulness for automatic readability assessment. In addition, the Margin-Infused Relaxed Algorithm is advantageous because it is an online algorithm and therefore allows for incremental training while still taking advantange of structural risk minimization.

3.1 Structural Risk Minimization

For many classification and regression problems, maximum margin approaches are shown to perform well with minimal amounts of training data. In general, these approaches involve linear discriminative classifiers that attempt to learn hyperplane decision boundaries which separate one class from another. Since multiple hyperplanes that separate classes can exist, these methods add an additional constraint: they attempt to learn hyperplanes while maximizing a region around the boundary called the margin. We show an example of this kind of margin in Figure 1, where the margin represents the maximum distance between the decision boundary and support vectors. The maximum margin approach helps prevent overfitting issues that can occur during training, a principle called structural risk minimization. Therefore we experiment with two such margin-maximizing algorithms, described below.

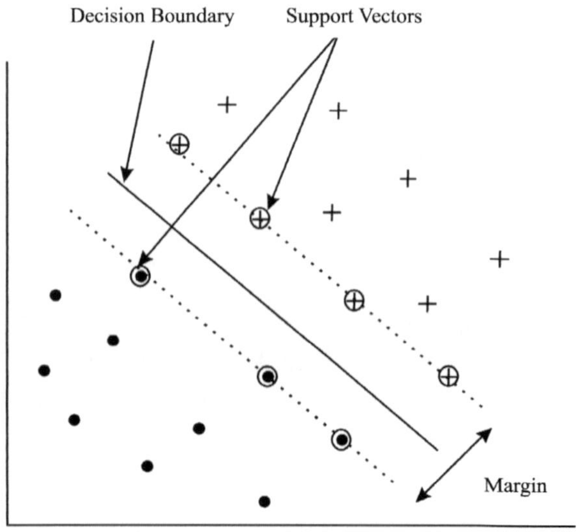

Figure 1: Graphical depiction of the maximum margin principle.

3.2 Support Vector Machines

For text classification problems, the most popular maximum margin approach is the SVM algorithm, introduced by Vapnik (1995). This approach uses a quadratic programming method to find the support vectors that define the margin. This is a batch training algorithm requiring all training data to be present in order to perform the optimization procedure (Joachims, 1998a). We used LIBSVM to implement our own SVM for regression (Chang and Lin, 2001).

Discriminative methods seek to best divide training examples in each class from out-of-class examples. SVM-based methods are examples of this approach and have been successfully applied to other text classification problems, including previous work on reading level assessment (Schwarm and Ostendorf, 2005; Petersen and Ostendorf, 2009; Feng et al., 2010). This approach attempts to explicitly model the decision boundary between classes. Discriminative methods build a model for each class c that is defined by the boundary between examples of class c and examples from all other classes in the training data.

3.3 Margin-Infused Relaxed Algorithm

Online approaches have the advantage of allowing incremental adaptation when new labeled examples are added during training. We implemented a version of MIRA from Crammer and Singer (2003), which we used for regression. Crammer and Singer (2003) proved MIRA as an online multiclass classifier that employs the principle of structural risk minimization, and is described as ultraconservative because it only updates weights for misclassified examples. For classification, MIRA is formulated as shown in equation (1):

$$c^* = \arg\max_{c \in \mathbf{C}} f_c(\mathbf{d}) \tag{1}$$

where

$$f_c(\mathbf{d}) = \mathbf{w} \cdot \mathbf{d} \tag{2}$$

and $\mathbf{w}$ is the weight vector which defines the model for class c. During training, examples are presented to the algorithm in an online fashion (i.e. one at a time) and the weight vector is updated according to the update shown in equation (2):

$$\mathbf{w}_t = \mathbf{w}_{t-1} + l(\mathbf{w}_{t-1}, \mathbf{d}_{t-1})\mathbf{v}_{t-1} \tag{3}$$

$$l(\mathbf{w}_{t-1}, \mathbf{d}_{t-1}) = ||\mathbf{d}_{t-1} - \mathbf{w}_{t-1}|| - \epsilon \tag{4}$$

$$\mathbf{v}_{t-1} = (sign(||\mathbf{d}_{t-1} - \mathbf{w}_{t-1}||) - \epsilon)\mathbf{d}_{t-1} \tag{5}$$

where $l(\cdot)$ is the loss function, ϵ corresponds to the margin slack, and $\mathbf{v}_{t-1}$ is the negative gradient of the loss vector for the previously seen example $||\mathbf{d}_{t-1} - \mathbf{w}_{t-1}||$. This update forces the weight vector towards erroneous examples during training. The magnitude of the change is proportional to the $l(\cdot)$. For correct training examples, no update is performed as $l(\cdot) = 0$. In a binary classification task, MIRA attempts to minimize the loss function in (4), such that the magnitude of the distance between a document vector and the weight vector is also minimized.

However, unlike topic classification or classification of words based on their semantic class where the classes are generally discrete, the ILR levels lie on a continuum (i.e. level 2 >> level 1 >> level 0). Therefore we are more interested in using MIRA for regression because we want to compare the predicted value with the true real-valued label, rather than a class label. For regression, we can redefine the MIRA loss function as follows:

$$l(\mathbf{w}_t, \mathbf{d}_t) = |l_t - \mathbf{d}_t \cdot \mathbf{w}_t| - \epsilon \tag{6}$$

In this case, l_t is the correct value (in our case, ILR level) for training document $\mathbf{d}_t$ and $\mathbf{d}_t \cdot \mathbf{w}_t$ is the predicted value given the current weight vector $\mathbf{w}_t$. We expect that minimizing this loss function cumulatively over the entire training set will yield a regression model that can predict ILR levels for unseen documents.

This revised loss function results in a modified update equation for each online update of the MIRA weight vector (generating a new set of weights $\mathbf{w}_t$ from the previously seen example):

$$\mathbf{w}_t = \mathbf{w}_{t-1} + l(\mathbf{w}_{t-1}, \mathbf{d}_{t-1})\mathbf{v}_{t-1} \tag{7}$$

$$\mathbf{v}_{t-1} = (sign(|l_{t-1} - \mathbf{d}_{t-1} \cdot \mathbf{w}_{t-1}|) - \epsilon)\mathbf{d}_{t-1} \tag{8}$$

$\mathbf{v}_{t-1}$ defines the direction of loss and the magnitude of the update relative to the current training example $\mathbf{d}_{t-1}$. Since this approach is online, MIRA does not guarantee minimal loss or maximum margin constraints for all of the training data. However, in practice, these methods perform as well as their SVM counterparts without the need for batch training (Crammer et al., 2006).

4 Experiments

4.1 Data

All of our experiments used data from four languages: Arabic (AR), Dari (DAR), English (EN), and Pashto (PS). In Table 2, we show the distribution of number of documents per ILR level for each language. All of our data was obtained from the Directorate of Language Science and Technology (LST) and the Language Technology Evaluation and Application Division (LTEA) at the Defense Language Institute Foreign Language Center (DLIFLC). The data was compiled using an online resource (Domino). Language experts (native speakers) used various texts from the Internet which they considered to be authentic material and they created the Global Language Online Support System (GLOSS) system. The texts were used to debug the GLOSS system and to see how well GLOSS worked for the respective languages. Each of the texts were labeled by two independent linguists expertly trained in ILR level scoring. The ratings from these two linguists were then adjudicated by a third linguist. We used the resulting adjudicated labels for our training and evaluation.

We preprocessed the data by doing the following tokenization: removed extra whitespace, normalized URIs, normalized currency, normalized

Level	AR	DAR	EN	PS
1	204	197	198	197
1+	200	197	197	199
2	199	201	204	200
2+	199	194	196	198
3	198	195	202	198
3+	194	194	198	200
4	198	195	190	195
Overall	1394	1375	1390	1394

Table 2: Total collection documents per language per ILR level.

numbers, normalized abbreviations, normalized punctuation, and folded to lowercase. We identified words by splitting text on whitespace and we identified sentences by splitting text on punctuation.

4.2 Features

It is necessary to define a set of features to help the regressors distinguish between the ILR levels. We conducted our experiments using two different types of features: word-usage features and shallow length features. Shallow length features are shown to be useful in reading level prediction tasks (Feng et al., 2010). Word-usage features, such as the ones used here, are meant to capture some low-level topical differences between ILR levels.

Word-usage features: Word frequencies (or weighted word frequencies) are commonly used as features for topic classification problems, as these features are highly correlated with topics (e.g. words like *player* and *touchdown* are very common in documents about topics like *football*, whereas they are much less common in documents about *opera*). We used TF-LOG weighted word frequencies on bag-of-words for each document.

Length features: In addition to word-usage, we added three z-normalized length features: (1) average sentence length (in words) per document, (2) number of words per document, and (3) average word length (in characters) per document. We used these as a basic measure of language level complexity. These features are easily computed by automatic means, and they capture some of the structural differences between the ILR levels.

Figures 2, 3, 4, and 5 show the z-normalized average word count per sentence for Arabic, Dari, English, and Pashto respectively. The overall data set for each language has a normalized mean of

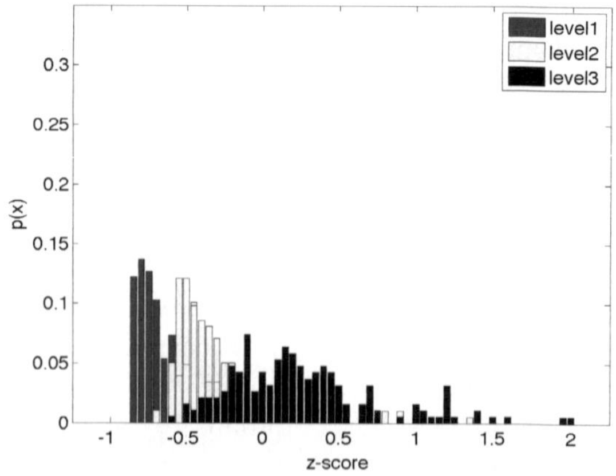

Figure 2: Arabic, z-normalized average word count per sentence for ILR levels 1, 2 and 3.

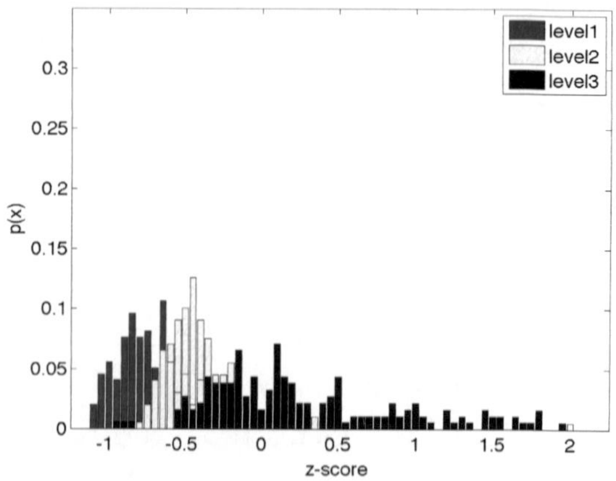

Figure 3: Dari, z-normalized average word count per sentence for ILR levels 1, 2 and 3.

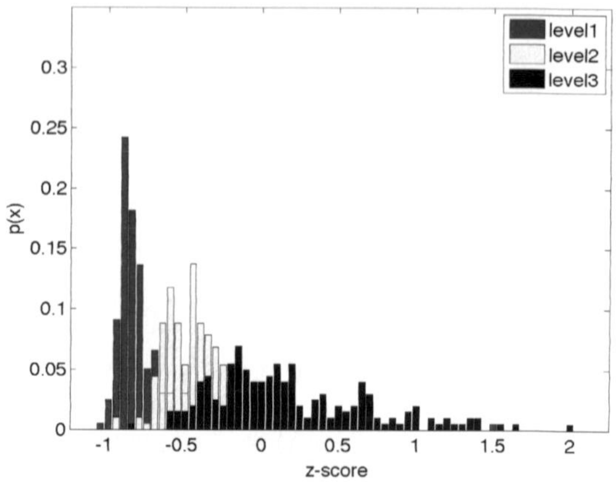

Figure 4: English, z-normalized average word count per sentence for ILR levels 1, 2 and 3.

	MIRA			SVM (linear)		
	LEN	WORDS	COMBINED	LEN	WORDS	COMBINED
AR	4.527	0.283	**0.222**	0.411	0.263	**0.198**
DAR	5.538	0.430	**0.330**	0.473	0.409	**0.301**
EN	5.155	0.181	**0.148**	0.430	0.181	**0.147**
PS	5.371	0.410	**0.360**	1.871	0.393	**0.391**

Table 3: Performance results (MSE) for SVM and MIRA on Arabic, Dari, English and Pashto for three different kinds of features/combinations.

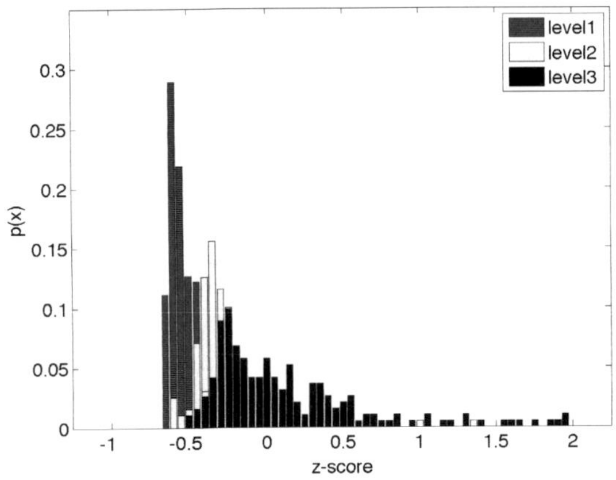

Figure 5: Pashto, z-normalized average word count per sentence for ILR levels 1, 2 and 3.

zero and unit variance, which were calculated separately for a given length feature. The x-axis shows the deviation of documents relative to the data set mean, in units of overall standard deviation. It is clear from the separability of the levels in these figures that sentence length could be an important indicator of ILR level, though no feature is a perfect discriminator. This is indicated by the significant overlap between the distributions of document lengths at different ILR levels.

4.3 Training

We split the data between training and testing using an 80/20 split of the total data for each language. To formulate the ILR scale as continuous-valued, we assumed that "+" levels are 0.5 higher than their basis (e.g. 2+ = 2.5). Though this may not be optimal if distances between levels are non-constant, the best systems in our experiments show good prediction performance using this assumption.

Both of the classifiers were trained to predict the ILR value as a continuous value using regression. We measured the performance of each method in terms of the mean squared error on the unseen test documents. We tested the following three conditions: length-based features only (LEN), word-usage features only (WORDS), and word and length features combined (COMBINED). Since each algorithm (SVM and MIRA) has a number of parameters that can be tuned to optimize performance, we report results for the best settings for each of the algorithms. These settings were determined by sweeping parameters to optimize performance on the training data for a range of values, for both MIRA and SVM. For both algorithms, we varied the number of training iterations from 500 to 3100 for each language, with stepsize of 100. We also varied the minimum word frequency count from 2 to 26, with stepsize 1. For MIRA only, we varied the slack parameter from 0.0005 to 0.0500, with stepsize 0.00025. For SVM (linear kernel only), we varied the C parameter and γ at a coarse setting of 2^n with values of n ranging from -15 to 6 with stepsize 1.

5 Results

We compared the performance of the online MIRA approach with the SVM-based approach. Table 3 shows the overall performance of MIRA regression and SVM regression, respectively, for the combinations of features for each language. Mean squared error was averaged over all of the levels in a given language. MIRA is an approximation to SVM, however one of the advantages of MIRA is that it is an online algorithm so it is adaptable after training and training can be enhanced later with more data with a small number of additional data points.

Figures 6 and 7 show the per-level performance for each classifier with the overall best features (COMBINED) for each language. The highest level (Level 4) and lowest levels (Level 1) tend to exhibit the worst performance across all languages for each regression method. Poorer performance on the outlying levels could be due to overfitting for both SVM and MIRA on those levels. The ILR scale includes 4 major levels at half-step intervals between each one. We are not sure if using a different scale, such as grade levels ranging from 1 to 12, would also exhibit poorer performance on the outlying levels because the highest ILR level corresponds to native-like fluency. This U-shaped performance is seen across both classifiers for each of the languages.

6 Analysis

Our results show that SVM slightly outperformed MIRA for all of the languages. We believe that the reason why MIRA performed worse than SVM is because it was overfit during training whereas SVM was not. This could be due to the parameters that we set during our sweep in training. We selected C and γ as parameters to SVM linear-kernel for the best performance. The γ values for English and Arabic were set at more than 1000 times smaller than the values for Pashto and Dari (AR:γ=6.1035156 $\times$ 10^{-}5, DAR:γ=0.0078125, EN:γ=3.0517578 $\times$ 10^{-}5, PS:γ=0.03125). This means that the margins for Pashto and Dari were set to be larger respective to English and Arabic. One reason why these margins were larger is because the features that we used had more discriminative power for English and Arabic. In fact, both MIRA and SVM performed worse on Pashto and Dari.

Since the method described here makes use of

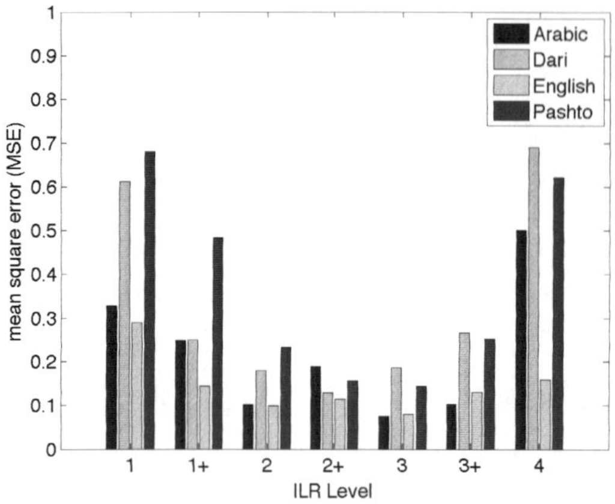

Figure 6: MIRA performance (MSE) per ILR level for each language.

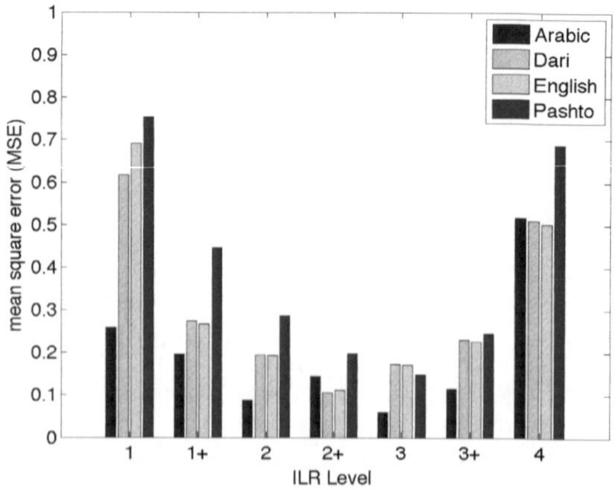

Figure 7: SVM performance (MSE) per ILR level for each language.

linear classifiers that weigh word-usage and length features, it is possible to examine the weights that a classifier learns during training to see which features the algorithm deems most useful in discriminating between ILR levels. One way to do this is to use a multiclass classifier on our data for the categorical levels (e.g. 1, 1+, 2, etc.) and examine the weights that were generated for each class. MIRA is formulated to be a multiclass classifier so we examined its weights for the features. We chose MIRA instead of SVM, even though LIBSVM supports multiclass classification, because we wanted to capture differences between levels which we could not do with one vs. all. We examined classifier weights of greatest magnitude to see which features were the most indicative and most contra-indicative for that level. We report these two types of features for Level 3 and Level 4 in Tables 4 and 5, respectively. Level 3 documents can have some complex topics, such as *politics* and *art*, however it can be noted that some of the more abstract topics like *love* and *hate* are contra-indicative of Level 3. On the other hand, we see that abstract topics are highly indicative Level 4 documents where topics such as *philosophy*, *religion*, *virtue*, *hypothesis*, and *theory* are discussed. We also note that *moral* is highly contra-indicative of Level 3 but is highly indicative of Level 4.

7 Discussion and Future Work

We have presented an approach to score documents based on their ILR level automatically using language-independent features. Measures of structural complexity like the length-based fea-

Most Indicative	+	Most Contra-Indicative	-
obama	1.739	said	-2.259
to	1.681	your	-1.480
republicans	1.478	is	-1.334
?	1.398	moral	-0.893
than	1.381	this	-0.835
more	1.365	were	-0.751
cells	1.355	area	-0.751
american	1.338	love	-0.730
americans	1.335	says	-0.716
art	1.315	hate	-0.702
it's	1.257	against	-0.682
could	1.180	people	-0.669
democrats	1.143	body	-0.669
as	1.139	you	-0.666
a	1.072	man	-0.652
but	1.041	all	-0.644
america	0.982	over	-0.591

Table 4: Dominant features for English at ILR Level 3.

Most Indicative	+	Most Contra-Indicative	-
of	3.298	+number+	-2.524
this	2.215	.	-2.514
moral	1.880	government	-1.120
philosophy	1.541	have	-1.109
is	1.242	people	-1.007
theory	1.138	would	-0.909
in	1.131	could	-0.878
absolute	1.034	after	-0.875
religion	1.011	you	-0.874
hyperbole	0.938	,"	-0.870
mind	0.934	were	-0.827
as	0.919	was	-0.811
hypothesis	0.904	years	-0.795
schelling	0.883	your	-0.747
thought	0.854	americans	-0.746
virtue	0.835	at	-0.745
alchemy	0.828	they	-0.720

Table 5: Dominant features for English at ILR Level 4.

tures used in this work are important to achieving good ILR prediction performance. We intend to investigate further measures that could improve this baseline, including features from automatic parsers or unsupervised morphology to measure syntactic complexity. Here we have shown that higher reading levels in English correspond more with abstract topics. In future work, we also want to capture some of the stylistic features of text, such as the complexity of dialogue exchanges.

For both SVM and MIRA, the combination of length and word-usage features had the best impact on performance across languages. We found better performance on this task overall for SVM and we believe that MIRA was overfitting during training. For MIRA, this is likely due to an interaction between a small number of features and the stopping criterion (mean squared error = 0) that we used in training, which tends to overfit. We intend to investigate the stopping criterion in future work. Still, we have shown that MIRA can be useful in this task because it is an online algorithm, and it allows for incremental training and active learning.

Our current approach can be quickly adapted for a new subset of languages because the features that we used here were language-independent. We plan to build a flexible architecture that enables language-specific feature extraction to be combined with our method so that these techniques can be easily used for new languages. We will continuously improve this baseline using the approaches described in this paper. We found that these two algorithms along with these types of features performed pretty well on 4 different languages. It is surprising that these features would correlate across languages even though there are individual differences between each language. In future work, we are interested to look deeper into the nature of language-independence for this task.

With respect to content, we are interested to find out if more word features are needed for some languages but not others. There could be diversity of vocabulary at higher ILR levels, which we could measure with entropy. Additionally, since the MIRA classifier that we are using is an online classifier with weight vector representation for each feature, we could examine the weights and measure the mutual information by ILR level above a certain threshold to find which features are the most predictive of an ILR level, for each language. Lastly, we have assumed that the ILR rating metric is approximately linear, and although we have used linear classifiers in this task, we are interested to learn if other transformations would give us a better sense of ILR level discrimination.

References

Chih-Chung Chang and Chih-Jen Lin. 2001. LIBSVM: a library for support vector machines. Software available at http://www.csie.ntu.edu.tw/~cjlin/libsvm.

Koby Crammer and Yoram Singer. 2003. Ultraconservative Online Algorithms for Multiclass Problems. *Journal of Machine Learning Research*, 3(2003):951-991.

Koby Crammer, Ofer Dekel, Joseph Keshet, Shai Shalev-Shwartz, and Yoram Singer. 2006. Online Passive-Agressive Algorithms. *Journal of Machine Learning Research*, 7(2006):551-585.

George R. Doddington, Mark A. Przybocki, Alvin F. Martin, and Douglas A. Reynolds. 2000. The NIST speaker recognition evaluation - overview, methodology, systems, results, perspective. *Speech Communication*, 31(2-3):225-254.

Lijun Feng, Martin Jansche, Matt Huenerfauth, Noémie Elhadad. 2010. A Comparison of Features for Automatic Readability Assessment. In *Proceedings of the 23rd International Conference on Computational Linguistics: Posters*. Association for Computational Linguistics, 2010.

Rudolph Flesch. 1948. A new readability yardstick. *Journal of Applied Psychology*, 32(3):221-233.

Interagency Language Roundtable. ILR Skill Scale. http://www.govtilr.org/Skills/ILRscale4.htm, 2013. Accessed February 27, 2013.

Thorsten Joachims. 1998a. Text categorization with support vector machines: learning with many relevant features. In *Proceedings of the European Conference on Machine Learning*, pages 137-142, 1998a.

Peter J. Kincaid, Lieutenant Robert P. Fishburne, Jr., Richard L. Rogers, and Brad S. Chissom. 1975. Derivation of new readability formulas for Navy enlisted personnel. Research Branch Report 8-75, U.S. Naval Air Station, Memphis, 1975.

Sarah E. Petersen and Mari Ostendorf. 2009. A machine learning approach to reading level assessment. *Computer Speech and Language*, 23(2009):89-106.

Sarah. E. Schwarm and Mari Ostendorf. 2005. Reading Level Assessment Using Support Vector Machines and Statistical Language Models. In *Proceedings of the 43rd Annual Meeting of the Association for Computational Linguistics*.

Kumiko Tanaka-Ishii, Satoshi Tezuka, and Hiroshi Terada. 2010. Sorting texts by readability. *Computational Linguistics*, 36(2):203-227.

Vladimir Vapnik. 1995. *The Nature of Statistical Learning Theory*. Springer, New York, 1995.

Text Modification for Bulgarian Sign Language Users

Slavina Lozanova* **Ivelina Stoyanova**† **Svetlozara Leseva**†
slavinal@abv.bg iva@dcl.bas.bg zarka@dcl.bas.bg
Svetla Koeva† **Boian Savtchev**‡
svetla@dcl.bas.bg bsavtchev@gmail.com
* AssistNet, Sofia, Bulgaria
† Department of Computational Linguistics, IBL, BAS, Sofia, Bulgaria
‡ Cambridge Language Assessment Centre BG015, Sofia, Bulgaria

Abstract

The paper discusses the main issues regarding the reading skills and comprehension proficiency in written Bulgarian of people with communication difficulties, and deaf people, in particular. We consider several key components of text comprehension which pose a challenge for deaf readers and propose a rule-based system for automatic modification of Bulgarian texts intended to facilitate comprehension by deaf people, to assist education, etc. In order to demonstrate the benefits of such a system and to evaluate its performance, we have carried out a study among a group of deaf people who use Bulgarian Sign Language (BulSL) as their primary language (primary BulSL users), which compares the comprehensibility of original texts and their modified versions. The results shows a considerable improvement in readability when using modified texts, but at the same time demonstrates that the level of comprehension is still low, and that a complex set of modifications will have to be implemented to attain satisfactory results.

1 Introduction

The individual development of deaf people depends on a complex of factors, which include the cause and the degree of hearing loss, the age of hearing loss onset, educational background, language and communication methods, cultural identification, disability preconceptions. Hearing loss leads to a limited spoken language input, delays in language acquisition and communication difficulties. Deaf children and adults demonstrate lower reading achievements than hearing people regardless of the degree of hearing loss, and the use (or lack) of high-performing hearing amplification devices (Paul, 1998; Conrad, 1979; Musselman, 2000; Traxler, 2000; Vermeulen AM, 2007), which shows that reading skills are influenced by complex social, linguistic and communication-related factors rather than by the sensory disability alone.

The paper explores reading comprehension of Deaf people[1] who use Bulgarian Sign Language (BulSL) as their primary language. Various research studies both in Bulgaria and abroad have shown that hearing-impaired BulSL users have poorer reading skills than their hearing peers. Various methods for text modification have been explored to the end of obtaining texts that correspond to the proficiency of the readers. Most of the modification methodologies have been focused on simplifying the original texts and decreasing their complexity (Inui et al., 2003). Our approach, however, focuses not on simplification, but on the adaptation of the structure of the original texts to the linguistic properties of BulSL.

The paper is organized as follows. Section 2 discusses the reading skills of BulSL users, paying attention to children's and adult education in Bulgaria focused on the acquisition of Bulgarian and the relationship between BulSL and verbal Bulgarian. After outlining the main principles which underlie text adaptation aimed at fostering text comprehensibility in the target population, we present a rule-based method for automatic modification of Bulgarian written texts. The method applies a set of linguistic transformations and produces modified versions of the texts, which are better suited to the needs of BulSL users (Section 3). Section 4 describes an experiment devised to explore the reading comprehension of BulSL users of original and modified texts. Section 5 draws conclusions

[1] Capitalized 'Deaf' is used to denote the community of deaf people who use Sign Language as their primary language. The term emphasizes the socio-cultural model of Deafness rather than the medical view of hearing impairment.

and outlines some directions for future work.

2 Reading Skills of Hearing-Impaired People

2.1 Education

Previous research has shown that deaf students lag behind their hearing peers in reading comprehension, because they experience difficulties with vocabulary (Paul, 1996), syntax (Kelly, 1996), and the use of prior knowledge and metacognition (Trezek et al., 2010). In addition, reading comprehension difficulties are often linked to lack of general knowledge due to inadequate education and limited access to information (Lewis and Jackson, 2001). Two independently performed studies (Albertini and Mayer, 2011; Parault and William, 2010) have found out that deaf college students' reading skills are below those of six-graders[2].

MacAnally et al. (1999) support the hypothesis that using less complicated and more accessible reading materials, consisting of language constructions close or similar to sign language structure can facilitate reading comprehension and motivate deaf people to read. In support of this claim Berent (2004) points out that deaf students would read more smoothly if the subject, verb, and object are in a simple SVO (subject-verb-object) word order. These studies provide evidence in favour of text adaptation that reflects features of the sign language and the development of modified teaching materials.

Bulgarian education for the deaf is based entirely on the oral approach and no systematic effort has been invested into exploring total communication and bilingual approaches (Lozanova, 2002; Saeva, 2010). Even in the specialized schools for the deaf, where sign language communication occurs naturally, BulSL has not been integrated into the school curriculum. Besides, the linguistic analysis of BulSL has been limited to mere descriptions and presentation of signs: Bulgarian Sign Language dictionaries (1966, 1996); Sign Language Dictionary in Civil Education (Stoyanova et al., 2003); Specialized Multimedia BulSL dictionary[3] (2005).

In order to improve education and the reading and communication skills of deaf people, a comprehensive study of BulSL is necessary, that will provide the basis for developing advanced methods for automatic text modification directed to improving text readability for deaf BulSL users.

2.2 Sign Language and Verbal Language

Research has shown that Deaf children of Deaf parents (DCDP) with sign language as their primary mode of communication outperform their deaf peers of hearing parents (DCHP) on different academic tests, including reading tests (Mayberry, 2000). Several studies have found a positive correlation between the advanced American Sign Language (ASL) skills of deaf students and their higher reading skills (Hoffmeister, 2000; Padden and Ramsey, 2000). Evidence is not conclusive as to how sign languages relate to verbal languages and what influence they have on the acquisition of general communication skills and knowledge about the world.

The extensive research on sign languages in the last fifty years worldwide has shown that they are independent linguistic systems which differ from verbal languages (Stokoe, 1960; Stokoe, 1972; Sutton-Spence and Woll, 2003). Being an independent language, a sign language affects the way in which its users conceptualize the world, according to the principle of linguistic relativity, first formulated by Sapir and Whorf (Lee, 1996). Due to the fact that sign languages are very different from verbal ones, many Deaf people attain a certain level of proficiency in a verbal language at the state of interlanguage[4] (Selinker, 1972) but that level is not sufficient to ensure successful social integration.

2.3 Readability of Written Texts for Native Users of Sign Language

Readability is measured mainly on the basis of vocabulary and sentence complexity, including word length and sentence length: the higher the letter, syllable and word count of linguistic units, the greater the demand on the reader. Some syntactic structures also affect readability – negative and interrogative constructions, passive voice, complex sentences with various relations between the main clause and the subordinates, long distance dependencies, etc. Besides, readability improves if the information in a text is well-organized and effec-

[2] 11-12-year-olds.

[3] http://www.signlanguage-bg.com

[4] The term 'interlanguage' denotes the intermediate state in second language acquisition characterized by insufficient understanding and grammatical and lexical errors in language production.

tively presented so that its local and global discourse structure is obvious to the reader (Swann, 1992).

Text modification is often understood as simplification of text structure but this may result in an inadequately low level of complexity and loss of relevant information. Moreover, using a limited vocabulary, avoiding certain syntactic structures, such as complex sentences, is detrimental to the communication and learning skills.

The efforts towards providing equal access to information for Deaf people lack clear principles and uniformity. Firstly, there is no system of criteria for evaluation of text complexity in terms of vocabulary, syntactic structure, stylistics and pragmatics. Further, no standard framework and requirements for text modification have been established, which limits its applications.

3 Text Modification of Bulgarian

Language modification for improved readability is not a new task and its positive and negative aspects have been extensively discussed (BATOD, 2006). One of the most important arguments against text modification is that it requires a lot of resources in terms of human effort and time. An appealing alternative is to employ NLP methods that will facilitate the implementation of automatic modification for improved readability of written texts aimed at the BulSL community.

3.1 General Principles of Text Modification

Several studies have observed different aspects of text modification: splitting chosen sentences with existing tools (Petersen and Ostendorf, 2007), 'translating' from complex to simplified sentences with statistical machine translation methods (Specia, 2010), developing text simplification systems (Candido et al., 2009), etc. (Siddharthan, 2011) compares a rule-based and a general purpose generator approaches to text adaptation. Recently the availability of the Simple English Wikipedia has provided the opportunity to use purely data-driven approaches (Zhu et al., 2010). The main operation types both in statistical and in rule-based approaches are: *change*, *delete*, *insert*, and *split* (Bott and Saggion, 2011).

Although text modification is a highly language dependent task, it observes certain general principles:

- Modified text should be identical or very close in meaning to the original.
- Modified text should be grammatically correct and structurally authentic by preserving as much as possible of the original textual and syntactic structure.
- In general, modified text should be characterized by less syntactic complexity compared with the original text. However, the purpose of the modification is not to simplify the text but rather to make the information in it more accessible and understandable by representing it in relatively short information chunks with simple syntax without ellipses.
- It should be possible to extend the range of modifications and include other components which contribute to readability or introduce other functionalities that facilitate reading comprehension, such as visual representations.

3.2 Stages of Text Modification

At present we apply a limited number of modifications: clause splitting, simplification of syntactic structure of complex sentences, anaphora resolution, subject recovery, clause reordering and insertion of additional phrases.

3.2.1 Preprocessing

The preprocessing stage includes annotation with the minimum of grammatical information necessary for the application of the modification rules. The texts are sentence-split, tokenized, POS-tagged and lemmatized using the Bulgarian Language Processing Chain[5] (Koeva and Genov, 2011). Subsequently, clause splitting is applied using a general method based on POS tagging, lists of clause delimiters – clause linking words and multiword expressions and punctuation, and a set of language specific rules.

We define a clause as a sequence of words between two clause delimiters where exactly one finite verb occurs. A finite verb is either: (a) a single finite verb, e.g. *yade* (*eats*); (b) or a finite verb phrase formed by an auxiliary and a full verb, e.g. *shteshe da yade* (*would eat*); or (c) a finite copular verb phrase with a non-verbal subject complement, e.g. *byaha veseli* (*were merry*).

We identify finite verbs by means of a set of rules applied within a window, currently set up to

[5]http://dcl.bas.bg/services/

two words to the left or to the right:

Rule P1. A single finite verb is recognized by the POS tagger. (Some smoothing rules are applied to detect the verb forms actually used in the context – e.g. forms with reflexive and negative particles).

Rule P2. If auxiliaries and a lexical verb form occur within the established window, they form a single finite verb phrase. (This rule subsumes a number of more specific rules that govern the formation of analytical forms of lexical verbs by attaching auxiliary verbs and particles.)

Rule P3. If an auxiliary (or a copular verb) but not a lexical verb form occurs within the established window, the auxiliary or copula itself is a single finite verb.

Rule P4. If a modal and/or a phase verb and a lexical verb form occur within the established window, they form a single finite verb phrase.

Rule P5. If a modal (and/or a phase) verb but not a lexical verb form occurs within the established window, the modal verb itself is a single finite verb.

A clause is labeled by a clause opening (CO) at the beginning and a clause closing (CC) at the end. We assume that at least one clause boundary – an opening and/or a close – occurs between any pair of successive finite verbs in a sentence. Each CO is paired with a CC, even if it might not be expressed by an overt element.

We distinguish two types of COs with respect to the type of clause they introduce: coordinate and subordinate. Most of the coordinating conjunctions in Bulgarian are ambiguous since they can link not only clauses, but also words and phrases. On the contrary, most of the subordinating conjunctions, to the exception of several subordinators which are homonymous with prepositions, particles or adverbs, are unambiguous.

Clause closing delimiters are sentence end, closing *comma*, *colon*, *semicolon*, *dash*.

The following set of clause splitting rules are applied (C1-C9):

Rule C1. The beginning of a sentence is a coordinate CO.

Rule C2. A subordinating clause linking word or phrase denotes a subordinate CO.

Rule C3. If a subordinate CO is on the top of the stack, we look to the right for a punctuation clause delimiter (e.g. comma) which functions as a CC element.

Rule C4. If a subordinate CO is on the top of the stack, and the CC is not identified yet, we look for a coordinating clause linking word or phrase which marks a coordinate CO.

Rule C5. If a coordinate CO is on the top of the stack, we look for another coordinating clause linking word or phrase which marks a coordinate CO.

Rule C6. If a coordinate CO is on the top of the stack and no coordinate CO is found, we look for a punctuation clause delimiter (e.g. a comma) which functions as a CC element.

Rule C7. If no clause boundary has been identified between two finite verbs, we insert a clause boundary before the second finite verb.

Rule C8. All COs from the stack should have a corresponding CC.

Rule C9. The part of the sentence to the right of the last finite verb until the end of the sentence should contain the CCs for all COs still in the stack.

3.2.2 Empty subject recovery

The detection, resolution, and assignment of function tags to empty sentence constituents have become subject of interest in relation to parsing (Johnson, 2002; Ryan Gabbard and Marcus, 2004; Dienes and Dubey, 2003), in machine translation, information extraction, automatic summarization (Mitkov, 1999), etc. The inventory of empty categories includes null pronouns, traces of extracted syntactic constituents, empty relative pronouns, etc. So far, we have limited our work to subject recovery.

A common feature of many, if not all, sign languages (BulSL among others) is that each sentence requires an overt subject. Moreover, each subject is indexed by the signer by pointing to the denoted person or thing if it is present in the signing area, or by setting up a point in space as a reference to that person or thing, if it is outside the signing area, and referring to that point whenever the respective person or object is mentioned. In order to avoid ambiguity, different referents are assigned different spatial points. Deaf people find it difficult to deal with complex references in written texts where additional disambiguating markers are rarely available. Being a pro(noun)-drop language, Bulgarian allows the omission of the subject when it is grammatically inferable from the context.

So far the following rules for subject recovery have been defined and implemented:

Rule SR1. In case the verb is in the first or second person singular or plural and the clause lacks a nominative personal pronoun that agrees with the finite verb, a personal pronoun with the respective agreement features is inserted in the text.
Rule SR2. In case the verb is in the third person singular or plural and the clause lacks a noun or a noun phrase that a) precedes the verb; and b) agrees with the verb in person, number and gender, the closest noun (a head in a noun phrase) in the preceding clause that satisfies the agreement features of the verb is inserted in the text. (The precision of the rule for singular verbs is low.)

3.2.3 Anaphora Resolution

With respect to text modification regarding anaphora resolution, we focus on a limited types of pronominal anaphors – personal, relative and possessive pronouns.

Bulgarian personal pronouns agree in gender and number with their antecedent. Possessive pronouns express a relation between a possessor and a possessed item, and agree both with their antecedent (through the root morpheme) and with the head noun (through the number and gender features of the inflection). For instance in the sentence *Vidyah direktora v negovata kola* (*I saw the director in his car*), the possessive pronoun *negov* indicates that the possessor is masculine or neuter singular and the inflection *-a* – that the possessed is feminine gender, singular. The agreement with the possessor is a relevant feature to text modification. Some relative pronouns *koyto* (*which*) (type one) agree with their antecedent in gender and number while others (type two) – *chiyto* (*whose*) agree with the noun they modify and not with their antecedent.

We have formulated the following rules for anaphora resolution:
Rule AR1. The antecedent of a personal or a possessive pronoun is the closest noun (the head in the noun phrase) within a given window to the left of the pronoun which satisfies the agreement features of the pronoun.
Rule AR2. The antecedent of a relative pronoun is the nearest noun (the head in the noun phrase) in the preceding clause that satisfies the agreement features of the pronoun.

The following rules for modification of anaphora can be used:
Rule R1. The third personal pronoun is replaced with the identified antecedent.
Rule R2. The possessive pronoun is replaced with a prepositional phrase formed by the preposition *na* (*of*) and the identified antecedent.
Rule R3. A relative pronoun of type one is replaced with the identified antecedent.
Rule R4. The relative pronoun *chiyto* (whose) is replaced with a prepositional phrase formed by the preposition *na* (of) and the identified antecedent.
Rule R5. The relative pronoun *kakavto* (*such that*) is replaced by a noun phrase formed by a demonstrative pronoun and the identified antecedent *takava chanta* (*that bag*).

3.2.4 Simplification of Complex Sentences

Complex sentences are one of the main issues for deaf readers because in BulSL, as well as in other sign languages, they are expressed as separate signed statements and the relation between them is explicit.

(Van Valin and LaPolla, 1997) observe that the elements in complex sentences (and other constructions) are linked with a different degree of semantic and syntactic tightness, which is reflected in the Interclausal Relations Hierarchy. The clauses in a sentence have different degree of independence, which determines whether they can be moved within the sentence or whether they can form an individual sentence.

Temporally related events in BulSL most often are represented in a chronological order, and the relation between them is expressed by separate signs or constructions (Example 1).

Example 1.
Zabavlyavayte se, dokato nauchavate i novi neshta.
Have fun while you learn new things.

Signed sentence:
Vie se zabavlyavate. Ednovremenno nauchavate novi neshta /ednovremenno/.
You have fun. Simultaneously, you learn new things /simultaneously/.
(the sign 'simultaneously' can be repeated at the end of the sentence again)

Chambers et al. (2007) and Tatu and Srikanth (2008) identify event attributes and event-event features which are used to describe temporal relations between events. Attributes include tense, grammatical aspect, modality, polarity, event class. Further, the event-event features include the following: *before*, *includes*, *begins*, *ends*, *simultaneously*, and their respective inverses (Chambers et al., 2007), as well as *sameActor* (binary feature indicating that the events share the same semantic role Agent), *eventCoref* (binary attribute capturing co-reference information), *oneSent* (true when both events are within the same sentence), *relToDocDate* (defining the temporal relation of each event to the document date) (Tatu and Srikanth, 2008).

(Pustejovsky et al., 2003) also introduce temporal functions to capture expressions such as *three years ago*, and use temporal prepositions (*for*, *during*) and temporal connectives (*before*, *while*). Three types of links are considered: TLINK (temporal link between an event and a moment or period of time); SLINK (subordination link between two events); and ALINK (aspectual link between aspectual types).

The structure of the complex sentences is simplified by clause reordering that explicitly reflects the chronological order of the described events. The preposition or postposition of clauses with temporal links *if*, *before*, *after*, etc. may not match the actual causal order. In such cases the order of clauses is simply reversed based on rules of the type:

Temporal link	*sled kato /when, after/*
Construction	CL1 temporal link CL2
Modification(s)	CL2. *Sled tova /then/* CL1.

3.2.5 Post-editing

Post editing aims at providing grammatically correct and semantically complete modified text. Clause reordering might lead to inappropriate use of verb tenses. Coping a subject from the previous sentence might require a transformation from an indefinite to a definite noun phrase. Thus, several checks for grammaticality and text cohesion are performed and relevant changes to verb forms and noun definiteness are made. Specific expressions are introduced to highlight temporal, causative, conditional and other relations and to serve as connectives.

Example 2 shows a fully modified text.

Example 2.

Original:

Vaz osnova na doklada ot razsledvaneto, sled kato litseto e bilo uvedomeno za vsichki dokazatelstva i sled kato e bilo izslushano, organat e izdal razreshenie.

Based on the report from the investigation, after the person has been notified about all evidence and after /he/ has been heard, the authorities have issued a permit.

Modified:

Litseto e bilo uvedomeno za vsichki dokazatelstva.
Litseto e bilo izslushano.
***Sled tova** vaz osnova na doklada ot razsledvaneto, organat mozhe da dade razreshenie.*

The person has been notified about all evidence.
The person has been heard.
***After that** based on the report from the investigation, the authorities may issue a permit.*

3.3 Evaluation of System Performance

The evaluation of performance is based on the Bulgarian part of the Bulgarian-English Clause-Aligned Corpus (Koeva et al., 2012) which amounts to 176,397 tokens and includes several categories: administrative texts, fiction, news. The overall evaluation of the system performance is assessed in terms of the evaluation of all subtasks (Section 3.2) as presented in Table 1. The evaluation of finite verbs and anaphora recognition, as well as subject identification is performed manually on a random excerpt of the corpus. Clause splitting is evaluated on the basis of the manual annotation of the corpus. We assess the precision and recall in terms of full recognition and partial recognition. In the first case the entire verb phrase, clause, anaphora, or dropped subject is recognized correctly, while in the latter – only a part of the respective linguistic item is identified. We account for partial recognition since it is often sufficient to produce correct overall results, e.g. partial verb phrase recognition in most cases yields correct clause splitting.

4 Experiments and Evaluation of Readability of Modified Texts

4.1 Outline of the Experiment

4.1.1 Aims and Objectives

The objective of the experiment was to conduct a pilot testing of original and modified texts in order

Task	Precision	Recall	F_1
Finite verb phrases (full)	0.914	0.909	0.912
Finite verb phrases (partial)	0.980	0.975	0.977
Clauses borders	0.806	0.827	0.817
Clauses (beginning)	0.908	0.931	0.919
Anaphora (full)	0.558	0.558	0.558
Anaphora (partial)	0.615	0.615	0.615
Subject (full)	0.590	0.441	0.504
Subject (partial)	0.772	0.548	0.671

Table 1: Evaluation of different stages of text modification

to determine and confirm the need of text modification for deaf people whose primary language is BulSL and the verbal language is acquired as a second language.

The rationale was to identify and distinguish between levels of comprehension of original and automatically modified texts.

4.1.2 Respondents' Profile

The participants were selected regardless of their degree and onset of hearing loss. The experiment targeted the following group of people:

- Socially active adults (18+);
- BulSL users;
- People with developed reading skills.

4.2 Pilot Test Design Methodology and Implementation

4.2.1 Text Selection

We decided to use original and modified versions of journalistic (e.g. news items) and administrative (e.g. legal) texts. The guiding principle was to select texts that are similar in terms of length, complexity, and difficulty.

The selected news refer to topics of general interest such as politics in neighbouring countries, culture, etc. The administrative texts represent real-life scenarios, rather than abstract or rare legal issues. In general, selected texts do not include domain-specific terms and professional jargon.

Regarding text modification the main objective was to preserve the meaning of the original text in compliance with the principles of textual and factual accuracy and integrity, and appropriate complexity. The result from the automatic modifications has been manually checked and post-edited to ensure grammaticality.

4.2.2 Methodology

The testing is conducted either online via tests in e-form (predominantly), or using paper-based versions. Respondents are given texts of each type, i.e. two original and two modified texts. Each text is associated with two tasks, which have to be completed correctly after the reading. The tasks seek to check the level of understanding of the main idea, details, purpose, implication, temporal relations (the sequence of events), and the ability to follow the text development.

- **Task-type 1: Sequence questions.** The respondents have to arrange text elements (sentences and clauses) listed in a random sequence into a chronological order. The task covers temporal, causative, conditional, and other relations, and its goal is to test reading comprehension which involves temporal and logical relations and inferences.
- **Task-type 2: Multiple response questions (MRQ) for testing general reading comprehension.** MRQ are similar to Multiple choice questions (MCQs) in that they provide a predefined set of options, but MRQ allow any number and combinations of options.

Text	Type	Version	# sentences	# clauses	# temporal shifts
1	News	Original	2	6	2
2	News	Modified	5	6	0
3	Admin	Original	1	4	2
4	Admin	Modified	4	4	0

Table 2: Structure of the test

4.2.3 Structure of the Test

The test consists of four different texts, each of them with two subtasks – for checking the comprehension of temporal relations and the logical structure of the events in the text (type 1), and general comprehension (type 2).

The number of sentences, clauses and temporal shifts for each text is presented in Table 2.

4.3 Analysis of Results

19 deaf adults proficient in BulSL have taken part in the pilot test study. The results are presented in Table 3 and on Figure 1.

Task	Type	Version	correct	all	%
1.1	News	Original	5	19	26.32
2.1	News	Modified	9	19	47.37
3.1	Admin	Original	6	19	31.58
4.1	Admin	Modified	10	19	52.63
1.2	News	Original	7	19	36.84
2.2	News	Modified	9	19	47.37
3.2	Admin	Original	7	19	36.84
4.2	Admin	Modified	10	19	52.63

Table 3: Results of chronological order subtasks (1.1-4.1) and general comprehension subtasks (1.2-4.2)

We recognize the fact that the small number of respondents does not provide sufficient data to draw conclusions regarding the improvement of readability when using modified texts. However, the results show a significant improvement ($t = 2.0066$ with $p = 0.0485 < 0.05$) in the overall comprehension (chronological order and general understanding) when using the modified texts in comparison with the original texts.

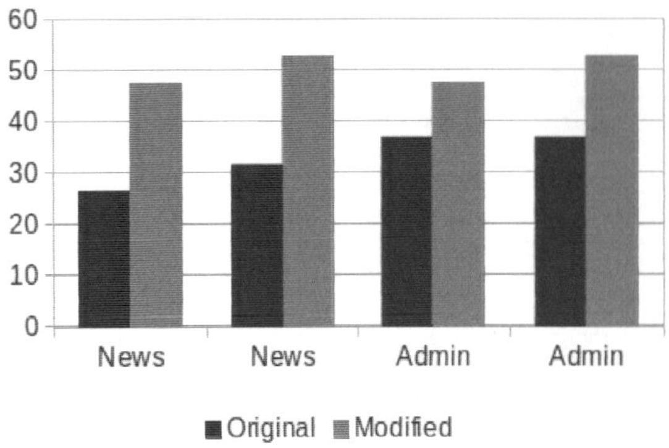

Figure 1: Results in % of correct answers for original and modified texts

Still, the improvement in readability after the text modification is very low and not sufficient to provide reliable communication strategies and access to information. Further work will be aimed at more precise methodology for testing the reading skills of deaf people.

5 Conclusions

As the pilot test suggests, the limited number of modifications is not sufficient to compensate for the problems which deaf people experience with reading. A wider range of text modifications are necessary in order to cover the problematic areas of verbal language competence. Other issues include the use of personal and possessive pronouns, in particular clitics, which are often dropped, the correct use of auxiliary verbs and analytical verb forms. Additional problems such as adjective and noun agreement, subject and verb agreement, etc. need to be addressed specifically, since these have a very different realization in sign languages (e.g., subject and verb are related spatially).

It should be emphasized that there has not been any systematic effort for studying BulSL so far. The detailed exploration of the linguistic properties of BulSL in relation to Bulgarian can give a deeper understanding about the problems in the acquisition of Bulgarian and in particular, the reading difficulties experienced by deaf readers.

Directions for future work include:

- To explore the relationship between reading comprehension and social, educational and other factors;
- To explore the dependence between reading skills and proficiency in BulSL;
- To analyze problems in relation to vocabulary with relation to reading;
- To build a detailed methodology for testing of reading comprehension;
- To explore further the potential of text modification with respect to BulSL in relation to the comparative analyses of the features of BulSL and verbal Bulgarian language.

References

J. Albertini and C. Mayer. 2011. Using miscue analysis to assess comprehension in deaf college readers. *Journal of Deaf Studies and Deaf Education*, 16:35–46.

BATOD. 2006. Training materials for language modification.

Gerald Berent. 2004. Deaf students' command of English relative clauses (Paper presented at the annual convention of Teachers of English to Speakers of Other Languages).

Stefan Bott and Horacio Saggion. 2011. Spanish text simplification: An exploratory study. In *XXVII Congreso de la Sociedad Espaola para el Procesamiento del Lenguaje Natural (SEPLN 2011), Huevla, Spain.*

Arnaldo Candido, Erick Maziero, Caroline Gasperin, Thiago A. S. Pardo, Lucia Specia, and Sandra Aluisio. 2009. Supporting the adaptation of texts for poor literacy readers: a text simplification editor for Brazilian Portuguese. In *Proceedings of the Fourth Workshop on Innovative Use of NLP for Building Educational Applications*, pages 34–42.

Nathanael Chambers, Shan Wang, and Dan Jurafsky. 2007. Classifying temporal relations between events. In *Proceedings of the ACL 2007 Demo and Poster Sessions, Prague, June 2007*, pages 173–176.

R. Conrad. 1979. *The deaf schoolchild*. London: Harper and Row.

Peter Dienes and Amit Dubey. 2003. Deep syntactic processing by combining shallow methods. In *Proceedings of the 41st Annual Meeting of the Association for Computational Linguistics*, volume 1.

R. J. Hoffmeister. 2000. A piece of the puzzle: ASL and reading comprehension in deaf children. In C. Chamberlain, J. P. Morford, and R. I. Mayberry, editors, *Language acquisition by eye*, pages 143–163. Mahwah, NJ: Earlbaum.

Kentaro Inui, Atsushi Fujita, Tetsuro Takahashi, Ryu Iida, and Tomoya Iwakura. 2003. Text simplification for reading assistance: A project note. In *PARAPHRASE '03 Proceedings of the second international workshop on Paraphrasing*, volume 16, pages 9–16. Association for Computational Linguistics Stroudsburg, PA, USA.

Mark Johnson. 2002. A simple pattern-matching algorithm for recovering empty nodes and their antecedents. In *Proceedings of the 40th Annual Meeting of the Association for Computational Linguistics.*

L. Kelly. 1996. The interaction of syntactic competence and vocabulary during reading by deaf students. *Journal of Deaf Studies and Deaf Education*, 1(1):75–90.

S. Koeva and A. Genov. 2011. Bulgarian language processing chain. In *Proceedings of Integration of multilingual resources and tools in Web applications. Workshop in conjunction with GSCL 2011, University of Hamburg.*

Svetla Koeva, Borislav Rizov, Ekaterina Tarpomanova, Tsvetana Dimitrova, Rositsa Dekova, Ivelina Stoyanova, Svetlozara Leseva, Hristina Kukova, and Angel Genov. 2012. Bulgarian-english sentence- and clause-aligned corpus. In *Proceedings of the Second Workshop on Annotation of Corpora for Research in the Humanities (ACRH-2), Lisbon, 29 November 2012*, pages 51–62. Lisboa: Colibri.

Penny Lee. 1996. *The Logic and Development of the Linguistic Relativity Principle. The Whorf Theory Complex: A Critical Reconstruction*. John Benjamins Publishing.

Margaret Jelinek Lewis and Dorothy Jackson. 2001. Television literacy: Comprehension of program content using closed-captions for the deaf. *Journal of Deaf Studies and Deaf Education*, 6(1):43–53.

Slavina Lozanova. 2002. Predpostavki za razvitie na bilingvizma kato metod za obuchenie na detsa s uvreden sluh. *Spetsialna pedagogika*.

R. I. Mayberry. 2000. Cognitive development of deaf children: The interface of language and perception in cognitive neuroscience. In *Child Neuropsychology, Volume 7 of handbook of neuropsychology*, pages 71–107. Amesterdam: Elsvier.

P. McAnally, S. Rose, and S. Quigley. 1999. *Reading practices with deaf learners*. Austin, TX: Pro-Ed.

Ruslan Mitkov. 1999. Anaphora resolution: the state of the art; working paper, (based on the coling'98/acl'98 tutorial on anaphora resolution).

Carol Musselman. 2000. How do children who can't hear learn to read an alphabetic script? a review of the literature on reading and deafness. *Journal of Deaf Studies and Deaf Education*, 5:9–31.

C. Padden and C Ramsey. 2000. American Sign Language and reading ability in deaf children. In C. Chamberlain, J. P. Morford, and R. I. Mayberry, editors, *Language acquisition by eye*, pages 165–189. Mahwah, NJ: Earlbaum.

S. J. Parault and H. William. 2010. Reading motivation, reading comprehension and reading amount in deaf and hearing adults. *Journal of Deaf Studies and Deaf Education*, 15:120–135.

Peter Paul. 1996. Reading vocabulary knowledge and deafness. *Journal of Deaf Studies and Deaf Education*, 1(1):3–15.

Peter Paul. 1998. *Literacy and deafness: The development of reading, writing and literate thought*. Needham, MA: Allyn & Bacon.

Sarah Petersen and Mari Ostendorf. 2007. *Natural language processing tools for reading level assessment and text simplification for bilingual education*. University of Washington Seattle, WA.

James Pustejovsky, José Casta no, Robert Ingria, Roser Saurí, Robert Gaizauskas, Andrea Setzer, Graham Katz, and Dragomir Radev. 2003. TimeML: Robust Specification of Event and Temporal Expressions in Text. Technical report, AAAI.

Seth Kulick Ryan Gabbard and Mitchell Marcus. 2004. Using linguistic principles to recover empty categories. In *Proceedings of the 42nd Annual Meeting on Association For Computational Linguistics*, page 184191.

S. Saeva. 2010. *Gluhota i Bilingvizam*. Aeropres BG.

L. Selinker. 1972. Interlanguage. *International Review of Applied Linguistics*, 10:209–231.

Advaith Siddharthan. 2011. Text simplification using typed dependencies: A comparison of the robustness of different generation strategies. In *Proceedings of the 13th European Workshop on Natural Language Generation (ENLG) , pages 211, September.*

L. Specia. 2010. Translating from complex to simplified sentences. In *9th International Conference on Computational Processing of the Portuguese Language (Propor-2010), Porto Alegre, Brazil*, volume 6001 of *Lecture Notes in Artificial Intelligence*, pages 30–39. Springer.

William Stokoe. 1960. Sign language structure: An outline of the visual communication systems of the american deaf. *Studies in linguistics: Occasional papers*, 8.

William Stokoe. 1972. *Semiotics and Human Sign Languages*. NICI, Printers, Ghent.

Ivelina Stoyanova, Tanya Dimitrova, and Viktorija Trajkovska. 2003. A handbook in civil education with a sign language dictionary. In *Social and Educational Training for Hearing Impaired youths: A Handbook in Civil Education with a Sign Language Dictionary*. Petar Beron, Sofia. (in Bulgarian).

Rachel Sutton-Spence and Bencie Woll. 2003. *The Linguistics of British Sign Language: An Introduction*. Cambridge University Press, 3rd edition.

W. Swann. 1992. *Learning for All: Classroom Diversity*. Milton Keynes: The Open University.

Marta Tatu and Munirathnam Srikanth. 2008. Experiments with reasoning for temporal relations between events. In *COLING '08 Proceedings of the 22nd International Conference on Computational Linguistics*, volume 1, pages 857–864.

C. B. Traxler. 2000. The stanford achievement test, 9th edition: National norming and performance standards for deaf and hard-of-hearing students. *Journal of Deaf Studies and Deaf Education*, 5:337348.

Beverly Trezek, Ye Wang, and Peter Paul. 2010. *Reading and deafness: Theory, research and practice.* Clifton Park, NY: Cengage Learning.

Robert Van Valin and Randy LaPolla. 1997. *Syntax: Structure, Meaning, and Function*. Cambridge University Press.

Schreuder R Knoors H Snik A. Vermeulen AM, van Bon W. 2007. Reading comprehension of deaf children with cochlear implants. *Journal of Deaf Studies and Deaf Education*, 12(3):283–302.

Zhemin Zhu, Delphine Bernhard, and Iryna Gurevych. 2010. A monolingual tree-based translation model for sentence simplification. In *Proceedings of The 23rd International Conference on Computational Linguistics, Beijing, China*, pages 1353–1361.

Modeling Comma Placement in Chinese Text for Better Readability using Linguistic Features and Gaze Information

Tadayoshi Hara[1] **Chen Chen**[2*] **Yoshinobu Kano**[3,1] **Akiko Aizawa**[1]
[1]National Institute of Informatics, Japan [2]The University of Tokyo, Japan
[3]PRESTO, Japan Science and Technology Agency
{harasan, kano, aizawa}@nii.ac.jp

Abstract

Comma placements in Chinese text are relatively arbitrary although there are some syntactic guidelines for them. In this research, we attempt to improve the readability of text by optimizing comma placements through integration of linguistic features of text and gaze features of readers.

We design a comma predictor for general Chinese text based on conditional random field models with linguistic features. After that, we build a rule-based filter for categorizing commas in text according to their contribution to readability based on the analysis of gazes of people reading text with and without commas.

The experimental results show that our predictor reproduces the comma distribution in the Penn Chinese Treebank with 78.41 in F_1-score and commas chosen by our filter smoothen certain gaze behaviors.

1 Introduction

Chinese is an ideographic language, with no natural apparent word boundaries, little morphology, and no case markers. Moreover, most Chinese sentences are quite long. These features make it especially difficult for Chinese learners to identify composition of a word or a clause in a sentence.

Punctuation marks, especially commas, are allowed to be placed relatively arbitrarily to serve as important segmentation cues (Yue, 2006) for providing syntactic and prosodic boundaries in text; commas indicate not only phrase or clause boundaries but also sentence segmentations, and they capture some of the major aspects of a writer's prosodic intent (Chafe, 1988). The combination of both aspects promotes cognition when reading text (Ren and Yang, 2010; Walker et al., 2001).

*The Japan Research Institute, Ltd. (from April, 2013)

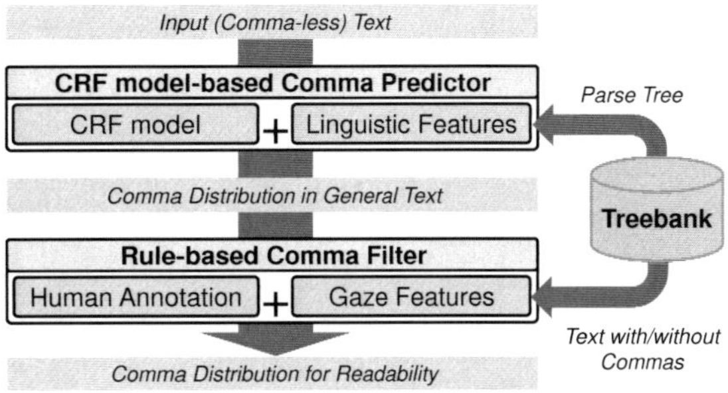

Figure 1: Our approach

However, although there are guidelines and research on the syntactic aspects of comma placement, prosodic aspects have not been explored, since they are more related with cognition. It is as yet unclear how comma placement should be optimized for reading, and it has thus far been up to the writer (Huang and Chen, 2011).

In this research, we attempt to optimize comma placements by integrating the linguistic features of text and the gaze features of readers. Figure 1 illustrates our approach. First, we design a comma predictor for general Chinese text based on conditional random field (CRF) models with various linguistic features. Second, we build a rule-based filter for classifying commas in text into ones facilitating or obstructing readability, by comparing the gaze features of persons reading text with and without commas. These two steps are connected by applying our rule-based filter to commas predicted by our comma predictor. The experimental results for each step validate our approach.

Related work is described in Section 2. The functions of Chinese commas are described in Section 3. Our CRF model-based comma predictor is examined in Section 4, and our rule-based comma filter is constructed and examined in Section 5 and 6. Section 7 contains a summary and outlines future directions of this research.

[Case 1] When a pause between a subject and a predicate is needed. (* (,) means the original or comparative position of the comma in Chinese text.) e.g. 我们看得见的星星，绝大多数是离地球非常远的恒星。(The stars we can see (,)* are mostly fixed stars that are far away from the earth.)
[Case 2] When a pause between an inner predicate and an object of a sentence is needed. e.g. 应该看到，科学需要一个人贡献出毕生的精力。(We should see that (,) science needs a person to devote all his/her life to it.)
[Case 3] When a pause after an inner (adverbial, prepositional, etc.) modifier of a sentence is needed. e.g. 对于这个城市，他并不陌生。(He is no stranger (,) to this city.) (The order of the modifier and the main clause is opposite in the English translation.)
[Case 4] When a pause between clauses in a complex sentence is needed, besides the use of semicolon (;). e.g. 据说苏州园林有一百多处，我到过的不过十多处。(It is said that there are more than 100 Suzhou traditional gardens, (,) no more than 10 of which I have been to.)
[Case 5] When a pause between phrases of the same syntactic type is needed. e.g. 学生比较喜欢年轻，有活力的教师 (The students prefer young (,) and energetic teachers.)

Table 1: Five main usages of commas in Chinese text

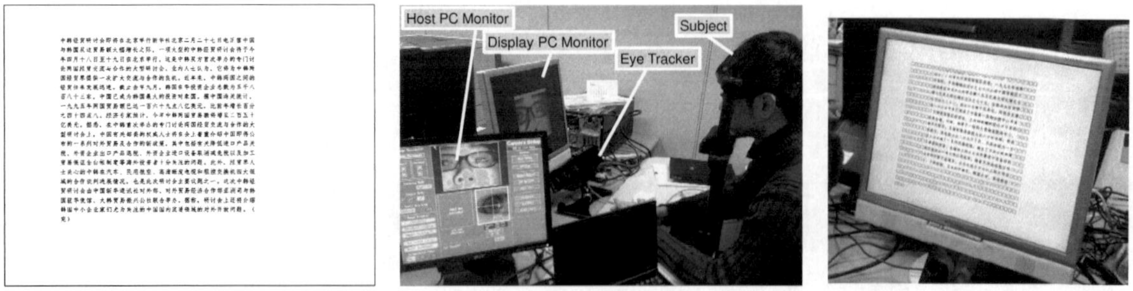

(a) Screenshot of a material (b) Scene of the experiment (c) Window around a gaze point

Figure 3: Settings for eye-tracking experiments

WS	Word surface
POS	POS tag
DIP	Depth of a word in the parse tree
STAG	Syntactic tag
OIC	Order of the clause in a sentence that a word belongs to
WL	Word length
LOD	Length of fragment with specific depth in a parsing tree

Table 2: Features used in our CRF model

```
((IP (PP (P 据)
     (NP (NN 了解)))
     (PU ，)
     (NP-TPC (CP (WHNP-1 (-NONE- *OP*))
         (CP (IP (NP-SBJ (-NONE- *T*-1))
              (VP (VV 新建)))
              (DEC 的)))
         (QP (CD 五)
         (CLP (M 家)))
         (NP (NN 保险)
         (NN 公司)) )
     (PU ，)
     (IP (IP (QP-SBJ (CD 三)
              (CLP (M 家)))
         (VP (VC 是)
         (DNP-PRD (ADJP (JJ 全国性))
               (DEG 的))))
     (PU ，)
     (IP (QP-SBJ (CD 两)
              (CLP (M 家)))
         (VP (VC 是)
         (DNP-PRD (ADJP (JJ 地区性))
               (DEG 的)))))
     (PU 。)))
```

(a)

```
WS|POS|STAG|DIP|OIC|WL|LOD|IOB-tag

据|P|PP|4|I0|1|1|O
了解|NN|NP|5|I0|2|3|B-Comma
*OP*|-NONE-|NP|6|C0|4|0|I-Comma
*T*-1|-NONE-|NP|8|I1|5|0|O
新建|VV|VP|8|I1|2|2|O
的|DEC|CP|6|C1|1|3|O
五|CD|QP|5|C0|1|4|O
家|M|CLP|6|C0|1|2|O
保险|NN|NP|5|I0|2|3|O
公司|NN|NP|5|I0|2|4|B-Comma
三|CD|QP|6|I2|1|5|I-Comma
家|M|CLP|7|I2|1|2|O
是|VC|VP|6|I2|1|2|O
全国性|JJ|ADJP|8|I2|3|3|O
的|DEG|DNP|7|I2|1|7|B-Comma
两|CD|QP|6|I2|1|5|I-Comma
家|M|CLP|7|I2|1|2|O
是|VC|VP|6|I2|1|2|O
地区性|JJ|ADJP|8|I2|3|3|O
的|DEG|DNP|7|I2|1|14|O
。|PU|IP|3|I1|1|27|O
```

(b)

Figure 2: Example of a parse tree (a) and its corresponding training data (b) with the features

2 Related Work

Previous work on Chinese punctuation prediction mostly focuses on sentence segmentation in automatic speech recognition (Shriberg et al., 2000; Huang and Zweig, 2002; Peitz et al., 2011).

Jin et al. (2002) classified commas for sentence segmentation and succeeded in improving parsing performance. Lu and Ng (2010) proposed an approach built on a dynamic CRF for predicting punctuations, sentence boundaries, and sentence types of speech utterances without prosodic cues. Zhang et al. (2006) suggested that a cascade CRF-based approach can deal with ancient Chinese prose punctuation better than a single CRF. Guo et al. (2010) implemented a three-tier maximum entropy model incorporating linguistically motivated features for generating commonly used Chinese punctuation marks in unpunctuated sentences output by a surface realizer.

3 Functions of Chinese Commas

There are five main uses of commas in Chinese text, as shown in Table 1. Cases 1 to 4 are from ZDIC.NET (2005), and Case 5 obviously exists in Chinese text. The first three serve the function of emphasis, while the latter two indicate coordinating or subordinating clauses or phrases.

In Cases 1 and 2, a comma is inserted as a kind of pause between a short subject and a long predicate, or between a short remainder predicate, such as 看到 (see/know), 説明/表明 (indicate), 発

Feature	F_1 (P/R)	A
WS	59.32 (72.67/50.12)	95.45
POS	32.51 (69.06/21.26)	94.08
DIP	34.14 (68.65/22.72)	94.13
STAG	22.44 (64.00/13.60)	93.67
OIC	9.27 (66.56/ 4.98)	93.42
WL	10.70 (75.24/ 5.76)	93.52
LOD	35.32 (59.20/25.17)	93.81
WS+POS	63.75 (79.93/53.01)	96.03
WS +DIP	70.06 (83.27/60.47)	96.61
WS +STAG	57.42 (81.94/44.19)	95.67
WS +OIC	60.35 (77.98/49.22)	95.73
WS +WL	60.90 (76.39/50.63)	95.71
WS +LOD	70.85 (78.87/64.31)	96.53
WS+POS+DIP	73.41 (84.62/64.82)	96.93
WS+POS+DIP+STAG	74.58 (83.66/67.27)	97.01
WS+POS+DIP +OIC	76.87 (84.29/70.65)	97.23
WS+POS+DIP +WL	70.18 (83.33/60.62)	96.63
WS+POS+DIP +LOD	76.61 (82.61/71.43)	97.16
WS+POS+DIP+STAG+OIC	76.62 (84.48/70.09)	97.21
WS+POS+DIP+STAG +WL	74.12 (84.00/66.33)	96.98
WS+POS+DIP+STAG +LOD	77.64 (85.11/71.38)	97.33
WS+POS+DIP +OIC+WL	75.43 (84.76/67.95)	97.11
WS+POS+DIP +OIC +LOD	78.23 (84.23/73.03)	97.36
WS+POS+DIP +WL+LOD	74.01 (85.80/65.06)	97.02
WS+POS+DIP+STAG+OIC+WL	77.25 (83.97/71.53)	97.26
WS+POS+DIP+STAG+OIC +LOD	77.31 (86.36/69.97)	97.33
WS+POS+DIP+STAG +WL+LOD	76.55 (85.24/69.46)	97.23
WS+POS+DIP +OIC+WL+LOD	77.60 (84.30/71.89)	97.30
WS+POS+DIP+STAG+OIC+WL+LOD	78.41 (83.97/73.54)	97.36

F_1: F_1-Score, **P**: precision (%), **R**: recall (%), **A**: accuracy (%)

Table 3: Performance of the comma predictor

Article ID	(A) #Characters,	(B) #Punctuations,	(C) #Commas	(C) / (A)	(C) / (B)	Subjects
6	692	49	28	4.04%	57.14%	L, T, C
7	335	30	15	4.48%	50.00%	L, T, C
10	346	18	7	2.02%	38.89%	L, T, C, Z
12	221	18	7	3.17%	38.89%	L, T, C
14	572	33	14	2.45%	42.42%	L, T, C
18	471	36	13	2.76%	36.11%	C, Z
79	655	53	28	4.27%	52.83%	Z
82	471	30	13	2.76%	43.33%	Z
121	629	41	19	3.02%	46.34%	Z
294	608	50	24	3.95%	48.00%	Z
401	567	43	21	3.70%	48.84%	L, T, C
406	558	39	18	3.23%	46.15%	Z
413	552	52	22	3.99%	42.31%	T, C, Z
423	580	49	26	4.48%	53.06%	L, C, Z
438	674	46	28	4.15%	60.87%	Z
Average	528.73	39.13	18.87	3.57%	48.22%	-

Table 4: Materials assigned to each subject

見 (find) etc., and following long clause-style objects. English commas, on the other hand, seldom have such usages (Zeng, 2006). In Cases 3 and 4, commas instead of conjunctions sometimes connect two clauses in a relation of either coordination or subordination. English commas, on the other hand, are only required between independent clauses connected by conjunctions (Zeng, 2006).

Liu et al. (2010) proved that Chinese commas can change the syntactic structures of sentences by playing lexical or syntactic roles. Ren and Yang (2010) claimed that inserting commas as clause boundaries shortens the fixation time in post-comma regions. Meanwhile, in computational linguistics, Xue and Yang (2011) showed

Figure 4: Obtained eye-movement trace map

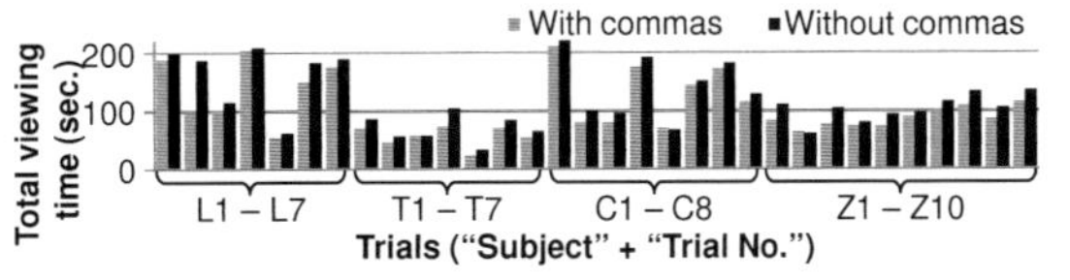

Figure 5: Total viewing time

that Chinese sentence segmentation can be viewed as detecting loosely coordinated clauses separated by commas.

4 CRF Model-based Comma Predictor

We first predict comma placements in existing text. The prediction is formalized as a task to annotate each word in a word sequence with an IOB-style tag such as I-Comma (following a comma), B-Comma (preceding a comma) or O (neither I-Comma nor B-Comma). We utilize a CRF model for this sequential labeling (Lafferty et al., 2001).

4.1 CRF Model for Comma Prediction

A conditional probability assigned to a label sequence Y for a particular sequence of words X in a first-order linear-chain CRF is given by:

$$P_\lambda(Y|X) = \frac{\exp(\sum_w^n \sum_i^k \lambda_i f_i(Y_{w-1}, Y_w, X, w))}{Z_0(X)}$$

where w is a word position in X, f_i is a binary function describing a feature for Y_{w-1}, Y_w, X, and w, λ_i is a weight for that feature, and Z_0 is a normalization factor over all possible label sequences.

The weight λ_i for each f_i is learned on training data. For f_i, the linguistic features shown in Table 2 are derived from a syntactic parse of a sentence[1]. The first three were used initially; the rest were added after we got feedback from construction of our rule-based filters (see Section 5). Figure 2 shows an example of a parsing tree and its corresponding training data.

[1]Some other features or tag formats which worked well in the previous research, such as bi-/tri-gram, a preceding word (L-1) or its POS (POS-1), and IO-style tag (Leaman and Gonzalez, 2008) were also examined, but they did not work that well, probably because of the difference in task settings.

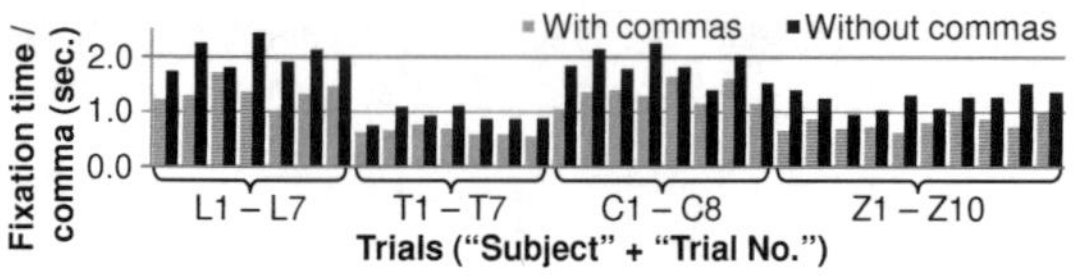

Figure 6: Fixation time per comma

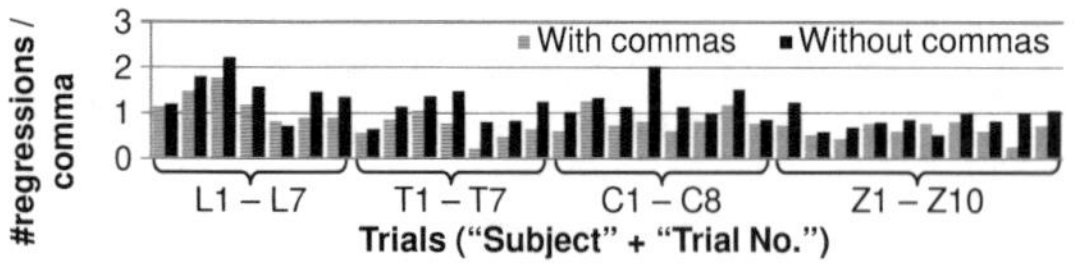

Figure 7: Number of regressions per comma

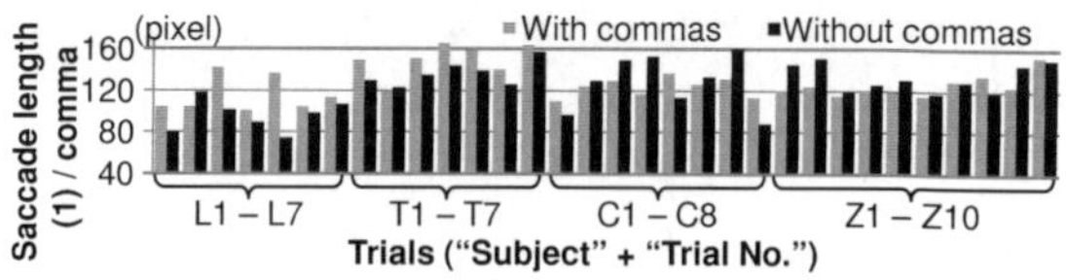

Figure 8: Saccade length (1) per comma

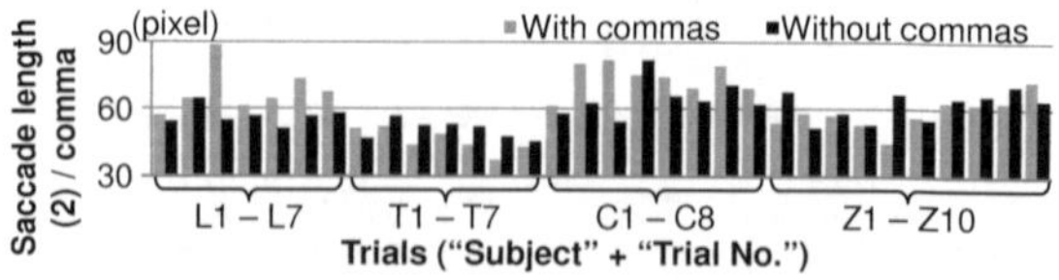

Figure 9: Saccade length (2) per comma

4.2 Experimental Settings

The Penn Chinese Treebank (CTB) 7.0 (Naiwen Xue and Palmer, 2005) consists of 2,448 articles in five genres. It contains 1,196,329 words, and all sentences are annotated with parse trees. We selected four genres for written Chinese (newswire, news magazine, broadcast news and newsgroups/weblogs) from this corpus as our dataset. These were randomly divided into training (90%) and test data (10%). We also corrected errors in tagging and inconsistencies in the dataset, mainly by solving problems around strange characters tagged as PU (punctuation). The commas and characters after this preprocessing numbered 63,571 and 1,533,928 in the training data and 4,116 and 111,172 in the test data.

MALLET (McCallum, 2002) and its application ABNER (Settles, 2005) were used to train the CRF model. We evaluated the results in terms of precision ($P = tp/(tp + fp)$), recall ($R = tp/(tp + fn)$), F_1-score ($F_1 = 2PR/(P+R)$), and accuracy ($A = (tp + tn)/(tp + tn + fp + fn)$), where tp, tn, fp and fn are respectively the number of true positives, true negatives, false positives and false negatives, based on whether the model and the corpus provided commas at each location.

4.3 Performance of the CRF Model

Table 3 shows the performance of our CRF model[2]. We can see that WS contributed much more to the performance than other features, probably because a word surface itself has a lot of information on both prosodic and syntactic functions. Combining WS with other features greatly improved performance, and as a result, with all features (WS + POS + STAG + DIP + OIC + LOD + WL), precision, recall, F_1-score and accuracy were 83.97%, 73.54%, 78.41 and 97.36%.

We also found that a large number of false positives seemed helpful according to native speakers (see the description of the subjects in Section 5 and 6). Although these commas do not appear in the CTB text, they might smoothen the reading experience. We constructed a rule-based filter in order to pick out such commas.

5 Rule-based Comma Filter

We constructed a rule-based comma filter for classifying commas in text into ones facilitating (positive) or obstructing (negative) the reading process as follows:

[Step 1]: Collect gaze data from persons reading text with or without commas (Section 5.1).

[Step 2]: Compare gaze features around commas to find those features that reflect the effect of comma placement. (Section 5.2).

[Step 3]: Annotate commas with categories based on the obtained features (Section 5.3), and devise rules to explain the annotation (Section 5.4).

5.1 Collecting Human Eye-movement Data

Eye-movements during reading contain rich information on how the document is being read, what the reader is interested in, where difficulties happen, etc. The movements are characterized by fixations (short periods of steadiness), saccades (fast movements), and regressions (backward saccades) (Rayner, 1998). In order to analyze the effect of commas on reading through the features, we collected gaze data from subjects reading text in the following settings.

[**Subjects and Materials**] Four native Man-

[2] Precision, recall, F_1-score, and accuracy with WS + POS + DIP + L-1 + POS-1 were 82.96%, 65.04%, 72.91 and 96.84%, respectively (lower than those with WS+POS+DIP).

Categories	Effect on readability	Outward manifestation
Positive (○)	Can improve readability.	Presence would cause GF+.
Semi-positive (△)	Might be necessary for readability, but the importance is not as obvious as a positive comma.	Absence might cause GF-.
Semi-negative (□)	Might be negative, but its severity is not as obvious as a negative comma.	Absence might cause GF+.
Negative (×)	Thought to reduce a document's readability.	Presence would cause GF-.

GF+/GF-: values of eye-tracking features that represent good/poor readability

Table 5: Comma categories

Subject	Positive (○)	Semi-positive (△)	Semi-negative (□)	Negative (×)	Adjustment formula
L	$\Delta FT'>800$	$500<\Delta FT'\leq 800$	$-100<\Delta FT'\leq 500$	$\Delta FT'<-100$	$\Delta FT' = \Delta FT + \Delta RT \times 200$
C	$\Delta FT'>900$	$600<\Delta FT'\leq 900$	$-200<\Delta FT'\leq 600$	$\Delta FT'<-200$	$\Delta FT' = \Delta FT + \Delta RT \times 275$
T	$\Delta FT'>600$	$300<\Delta FT'\leq 600$	$-300<\Delta FT'\leq 300$	$\Delta FT'<-300$	$\Delta FT' = \Delta FT + \Delta RT \times 250$
Z	$\Delta FT'>650$	$350<\Delta FT'\leq 650$	$-250<\Delta FT'\leq 350$	$\Delta FT'<-250$	$\Delta FT' = \Delta FT + \Delta RT \times 250$

ΔFT = [fixation time (without commas) [ms]] − [fixation time (with commas) [ms]]
ΔRT = [#regressions (without commas)] − [#regressions (with commas)]

Table 6: Estimation formula for judging the contribution of commas to readability

ID	○	△	□	×
6	13	6	4	5
7	8	6	1	0
10	5	0	1	1
12	1	4	2	0
14	4	4	5	1
18	5	1	4	3
79	11	4	9	4
82	5	6	2	0

ID	○	△	□	×
121	11	2	6	0
294	9	9	4	1
401	10	7	2	2
406	5	6	5	2
413	8	5	6	3
423	11	4	7	4
438	6	16	6	0
Total	112	80	64	26

Table 7: Categories of annotated commas

darin Chinese speakers (graduate students and researchers) read 15 newswire articles selected from CTB 7.0 (included in the test data in Section 4.2). Table 4 and Figure 3(a) show the materials assigned to each subject and a screenshot of one material. Each article was presented in 12-15 points of bold-faced Fang-Song font occupying 13×13, 14×15, 15×16 or 16×16 pixels along with a line spacing of 5-10 pixels[3].

[**Apparatus**] Figure 3(b) shows a scene of the experiment. An EyeLink 1000 eye tracker (SR Research Ltd., Toronto, Canada) with a desktop mount monitored the movements of a right eye at 1,000 Hz. The subject's head was supported at the chin and forehead. The distance between the eyes and the monitor was around 55 cm, and each Chinese character subtended a visual angle 1°. Text was presented on a 19" monitor at a resolution of 800×600 pixels, with the brightness adjusted to a comfortable level. The displayed article was masked except for the area around a gaze point (see Figure 3(c)) in order to confirm that the gaze point was correctly detected and make the subject concentrate on the area (adjusted for him/her).

[**Procedure**] Each article was presented twice (once with/once without commas) to each subject. The one without commas was presented first[4] (not necessarily in a row). We did not give any comprehension test after reading; we just asked the subjects to read carefully and silently at their normal or lower speed, in order to minimize the effect of the first reading on the second. The subjects were informed of the presence or absence of commas beforehand. The apparatus was calibrated before the experiment and between trials. The experiment lasted around two hours for each subject.

[**Alignment of eye-tracking data to text**] Figure 4 shows an example of the obtained eye-movement trace map, where circles and lines respectively mean fixation points and saccades, and color depth shows their duration. The alignment of the data to the text is a critical task, and although automatic approaches have been proposed (Martínez-Gómez et al., 2012a; Martínez-Gómez et al., 2012b), they do not seem robust enough for our purpose. Accordingly, we here just compared the entire layout of the gaze point distribution and that of the actual text, and adjusted them to have relatively coherent positions on the x-axis; i.e., the beginning and end of the gaze point sequence in a line were made as close as possible to those of the line in the text.

5.2 Analysis of Eye-movement Data

The gaze data were analyzed by focusing on regions around each comma or where each one should be (three characters left and right to the comma[5]).

[3]These values, as well as the screen position of the article, were adjusted for each subject.

[4]If we had used the reversed order, the subject would have knowledge about original comma distribution, and this would cause abnormally quick reading of the text without commas. With the order we set, conflicts between false segmentations (made in first reading) and correct ones might bother the subject, which is trade-off (though minor) in the second reading.

[5]When a comma appeared at the beginning of a line, two characters to the left and right of the comma and one charac-

1. If L_Seg and R_Seg are both very long, a comma must be put between them.
2. If two △ appear serially, one is necessary whereas the other might be optional or judged negative, but it still depends on the lengths of the siblings.
3. If two neighboring commas appear very close to each other, one of them is judged as negative whereas judgment on the other one is reserved.
4. If several (more than 2) ×s appear continually, one or more ×s might be reserved in consideration of the global condition.
5. A comma is always needed after a long sentence or clause without any syntactically significant punctuation with the function of segmentation.
6. If a △ appears near a ○, it might be judged as negative with a high probability. However, the judgment process is always from the bottom up, which means × → □ → △ → ○. For example, if a □ appears near a △, we judge □ first (to be positive or negative), then judge the △ in the condition with or without the comma of □.

Table 8: General rules for reference

Figure 5, 6 and 7 respectively show the total viewing time, fixation time (duration for all fixations and saccades in a target region) per comma, and number of regressions per comma[6] for each trial. We can see a general trend wherein the former two were shorter and the latter was smaller for the articles with commas than without. The diversity of the subjects was also observed in Figure 6.

Figure 8 and 9 show the saccade length per comma for different measures. The former (latter) figure considers a saccade in which at least one edge (both edges) was in the region. We cannot see any global trend, probably because of the difference in global layout of materials brought by the presence or absence of commas.

5.3 Categorization of Commas

Using the features shown to be effective to represent the effect of comma placement, we analyzed the statistics for each comma in order to manually construct an estimation formula for judging the contribution of each comma to readability. The contribution was classified into four categories (Table 5), and the formula is described in Table 6[7]. The adjustment formula was based on our observation that the number of regressions could only be regarded as an aid. For example, for subject C, if ΔFT=200ms and ΔRT $=-2$, ΔFT$'=-350$, and therefore, the comma is annotated as negative. All parameters were decided empirically and manually checked twice (self-judgment and feedback from the subjects).

On the basis of this estimation formula, all articles in Table 4 were manually annotated. Table 7 shows the distribution of the assigned categories[8].

ter to the left and right of the final character of the last line were analyzed.

[6]Calculated by counting the instances where the x-position of [a fixation / end point of a saccade] was ahead of [the former fixation / its start point]. Although the counts of these two types were almost the same, by counting both of them, we expected to cover any possible regression.

[7]One or two features are used to judge the category of a comma. We will explore more features in the future.

[8]In the case of severe contradictions, the annotators discussed them and resolved them by voting.

5.4 Implementation of Rule-based Filter

The annotated commas were classified into Cases 1 to 5 in Table 1, based on the types of left and right segment conjuncts (L_Seg and R_Seg, which were obtained from the parse trees in CTB). For each of the five cases, the reason for the assignment of a category (○, △, □ or ×) to each comma was explained by a manually constructed rule which utilized information about L_Seg and R_Seg. The rules were constructed so that they would cover as many instances as possible. Table 8 shows the general rules utilized as a reference, and Table 9 shows the finally obtained rules. The rightmost column in this table shows the number of commas matching each rule. These rules were then implemented as a filter for classifying commas in a given text.

For several rules (○10, □8, □10, □11 and □12), there were only single instances. In addition, although our rules were built carefully, a few exceptions to the detailed threshold were found. Collecting and investigating more gaze data would help to make our rules more sophisticated.

6 Performance of the Rule-based Filter

We assumed that our comma predictor provides a CTB text with the same distribution as the original one in CTB (see Figure 1). Accordingly, we examined the quality of the comma categorization by our rule-based filter through gaze experiments.

6.1 Experimental Settings

Another five native Mandarin Chinese speakers were invited as test subjects. The CTB articles assigned to the subjects are listed in Table 10. These articles were selected from the test data in Section 4.2 in such a way that 520<*#characters*<700, *#commas*>17, *#commas*/*#punctuations*>38%, and *#commas*/*#characters*>3.1%, since we needed articles of appropriate length with a fair number of commas. After that, we manually chose articles that seemed to attract the subjects' interest from those that satisfied the conditions.

Case 1: L_Subject + R_Predicate		#commas
○6	L_IP-SBJ + R_VP (length both<14 (In_Seg_Len))	2
△7	L_IP-SBJ/NP-SBJ (Org_Len>13, Ttl_Len>15)	7
×6	L_NP-SBJ/IP-SBJ (<14) + R_VP (≥25)	2
Case 2: L_Predicate + R_Object		**#commas**
○9	Long frontings (Modifier/Subject, >7) + short L_predicate (VV/VRD/VSB· · · , ≤3) + Longer R_object (IP-OBJ, >28)	6
△8	Short frontings (<5) + short L_predicate (<3) + moderate-length R_object (IP-SBJ, <20)	4
□6	Short frontings (<6) + short L_predicate (≤3) + long R_object (IP-SBJ, >23)	9
Case 3: L_Modifier		**#commas**
○3	Short frequently used L_modifier (2-3, 经…, 据…, etc.) + moderate-length/long R_SPO (≥w18p10)	13
○7	Short L_(PP/LCP)-TMP (5, 6) + long R_NP (≥10)	4
○10	Long L_CP-CND (e.g., 若…, >18) + moderate-length R_Seg (SPO, IP, etc. <18)	1
△1	Long L_modifier (PP(-XXX, P+Long NP/IP), IP-ADV, ≥17)	6
△4	Moderate-length/short L_modifier (PP(-XXX, P+IP, There is IP inside, >6<15, cf. □6 (NP))	9
△9	Long L_(PP/LCP)-TMP (Ttl_Len≥10), short R_Seg (NP/ADVP, <3)	4
△10	Short L_(LCP/PP)-LOC (<8)	2
□2	Long L_LOC (or there is LCP inside PP, >10)	5
□3	Very short frequently used L_ADVP/ADV (2)	8
□5	Short L_(PP/LCP/NP)-TMP (4;5-6, when R_Seg is short (<10))	12
□4	Moderate-length PP(-XXX, P+NP, >8 ≤13) + R_Seg (SPO, IP, VO, MSPO, etc.)	6
□8	Short L_IP-CND (<8)	1
□11	Long L_PP-DIR (>20) + short R_VO (≤10)	1
×2	Very short L_(QP/NP/LCP)-TMP (≤3)	8
×5	Short frequently used L_modifier (as in ○3, ≤3) + short/moderate-length R_Seg (SPO etc., <c20w9)	1
Case 4: L_c + R_c		**#commas**
○2	L_c & R_c are both long (In_Seg_Len≥15; or one>13, the other near 20)	39
○8	L_c is the summary of R_c	2
△2	Moderate-length L_c + R_c (both ≥10≤15; or one≥17, the other≤12)	25
△3	Moderate-length clause (>10), but connected with familiar CC or ADVP	6
△5	Three or more consecutive moderate-length clauses (all<15, and at least one ≤10)	12
×7	Very short L_c + R_c (both <5), something like slogan)	1
Case 5: L_p + R_p		**#commas**
○1	Short coordinate modifiers (Both side <5)	4
○4	Short L_p+R_p (both<c15w5, and at least one <10), but pre-L_p (e.g., SBJ) is too long (>18)	2
○5	Between two moderate-length/long phrases (both ≥15; or L_p≥17, R_p=10-14; Or L_p=10-14, R_p>20)	39
○11	Long pre-L_p (SBJ /ADV, etc. >16) + short L_p (≤5) + long R_p (≥18)	2
(△3	Moderate-length phrase (>10), but connected with familiar CC or ADVP)	(6)
△6	Three or more consecutive short/moderate-length phrases (both<15, at least one<8)	5
□1	Between short phrases (both ≤c13w5), and pre-L_p (SBJ/ADV, etc.) is short/moderate-length (<11)	13
□7	Coordinate VPs, and L_VP is a moderate-length VP (PP-MNR VP)	4
□9	Phrasal coordination between a long (≥18) and a short (<10) phrase	3
□10	Moderate-length coordinate VPs (>10<15), and R_VP has the structure like VP (MSP VP)	1
□12	Between two short/moderate-length NP phrases (both ≤15, e.g., L_NP-TPC+R_NP-SBJ)	1
×1	Moderate-length/short phrase ((i) c:one>10<18, The other >5≤10, w:one≤5, the other>5≤10; (ii) c:both≥10<15, w:both>5≤7), and pre-L_p (SBJ/ADV, etc.) is short (≤5)	13

· L_x/R_x: the left/right segment of a target comma which is x.
(x can be "p" (phrase) / "c" (clause), syntactic tags (with function tags) such as "VP" and "IP-SBJ", or general functions such as "Subject" and "Predicate".)
· Org_Len: the number of characters in a segment (including other commas or punctuation inside).
· In_Seg_Len/Ttl_Len: the number of characters between the comma and nearest punctuation (inside a long/outside a short target segment).
· SPO: subject + predicate + object, belonging to the outermost sentence. The length is defined in the similar way as In_Seg_Len.
· MSPO: modifier + subject + predicate + object. The length is defined in the similar way as In_Seg_Len.
· -XX or -XXX: arbitrary type of possible functional tag (or without any functional tag) connected with the former syntactic tag.
· $\leq ciwj$: #characters$\leq i$ and #words$\leq j$.
· In some cases (in Case 3, 4 and 5), the length is calculated after negative (or judged negative) commas are eliminated.
· The rules related with TMP are applied faster than ones related with LCP (in Case 3).
· △3 appears in both Case 4 (clause) and Case 5 (phrase). The number of commas is given by the sum of those in both cases.

Table 9: Entire classification of rules based on traditional comma categories

Article ID	(A) #Characters, (B) #Punctuations, (C) #Commas			(C) / (A)	(C) / (B)	Subjects
6	692	49	28	4.04%	57.14%	L, S, H
11	672	48	21	3.13%	43.75%	L, S, F
15	674	67	26	3.86%	38.81%	L, S, H
16	547	43	22	4.02%	51.16%	L, S, F
56	524	43	18	3.44%	41.86%	L, H, M
73	595	46	28	4.71%	60.87%	S, H, F, M
79	655	53	28	4.27%	52.83%	H, F, M
99	671	55	24	3.58%	43.64%	F, M
Average	628.75	50.50	24.38	3.88%	48.27%	-

Table 10: Materials assigned to each subject

Our rule-based filter was applied to the commas of each article[9], and the commas were classified into two distributions: a positive one (positive + semi-positive commas) and a negative one (negative + semi-negative commas). Two types of materials were thus generated by leaving the commas in one distribution and removing the others.

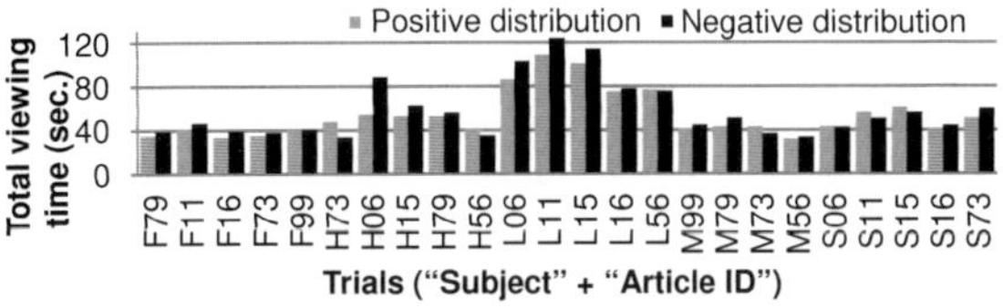

Figure 10: Total viewing time for two distributions

[9]Instances of incoherence among the applied rules were manually checked and corrected.

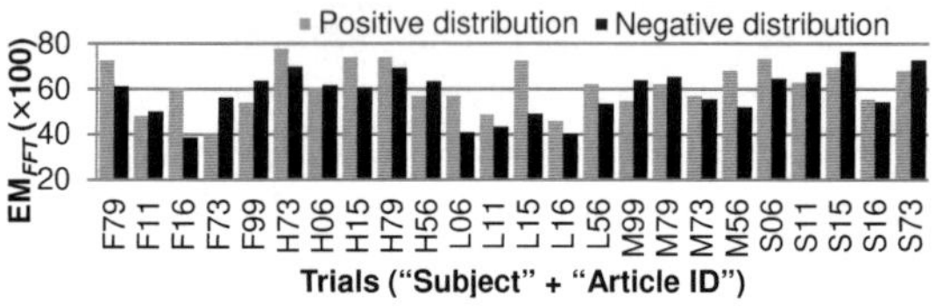

Figure 11: EM_{FFT} for two distributions

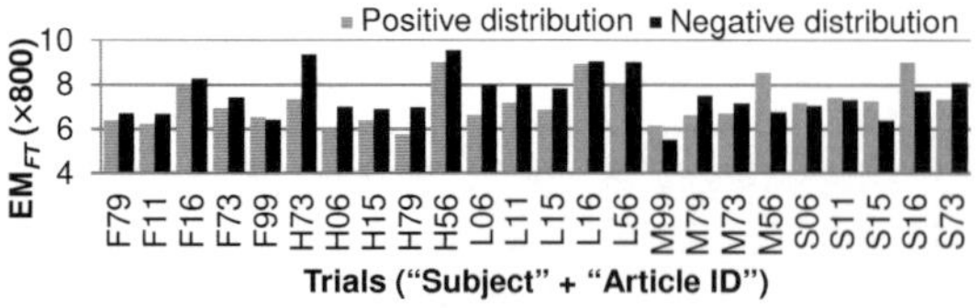

Figure 12: EM_{FT} for two distributions

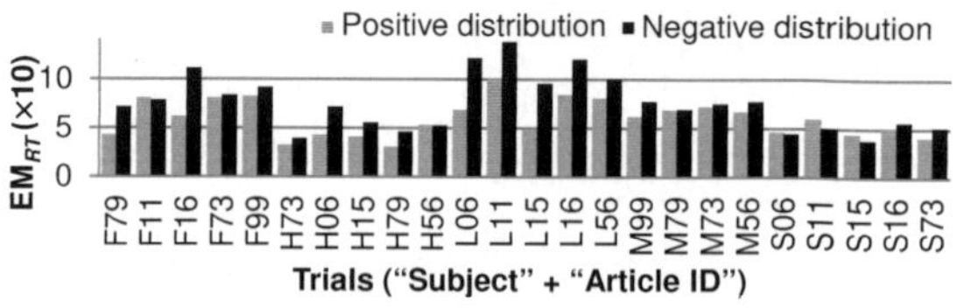

Figure 13: EM_{RT} for two distributions

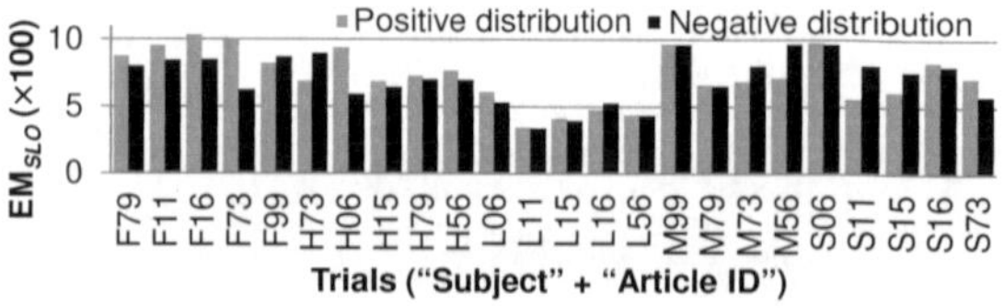

Figure 14: EM_{SLO} for two distributions

The apparatus and procedure were almost the same as those in Section 5.1, whereas, on the basis of the feedback from the previous experiments, the font size, number of characters in a line, and line spacing were fixed to single optimized values, respectively, 14-point Fang-Song font occupying 15×16 pixels, 33 characters and 7 pixels.

6.2 Evaluation Metrics

We examined whether our positive/negative distributions really facilitated/obstructed the subjects' reading process by using the following metrics:

TT, $\mathrm{EM}_{FFT} = \frac{\mathrm{FFT}}{\mathrm{FT}}$[10], $\mathrm{EM}_{FT} = \frac{\mathrm{FT}}{\mathrm{CN \cdot TT}}$[11], $\mathrm{EM}_{RT} = \frac{\mathrm{RT}}{2 \cdot \mathrm{CN}}$[12], $\mathrm{EM}_{\mathrm{SLO}} = \frac{\mathrm{SLO}}{2 \cdot \mathrm{TT}}$,

where TT, FT, RT and CN are total viewing time, fixation time, number of regressions, and number of commas respectively, as described in Section 5.2. FFT and SLO are additionally introduced metrics respectively for the "total duration for all first-pass fixations in a target region that exclude any regressions" and for the "length of saccades from inside a target region to the outside"[13]. All of the areas around commas appearing in the original article were considered target areas for the metrics. The other settings were the same as in Section 5.

6.3 Contribution of Categorized Commas

Figure 10, 11, 12, 13 and 14 respectively show TT, EM_{FFT}, EM_{FT}, EM_{RT} and EM_{SLO} for two types of comma distributions in each trial.

[10] Ratio to the total fixation time in the target areas (FT).

[11] Normalized by the total viewing time (TT).

[12] Two types of RT count (see Section 5.2) were averaged.

[13] Respectively to reflect "the early-stage processing of the region" and "the information processed for a fixation and a decision of the next fixation point" (Hirotani et al., 2006).

For TT, we cannot see any general trend, mainly because this time, the reading order of the text was random, which spread out the second reading effect evenly between the two distributions. For EM_{FFT}, we cannot reach a conclusion either. In contrast, in more than half of the trials, EM_{FFT} was larger for positive distributions, which would imply that the positive commas helped to prevent the reader's gaze from revisiting the target regions. For most trials, except for subject S whose calibration was poor and reading process was poor in M56, EM_{FT} and EM_{RT} decreased and EM_{SLO} increased for positive distributions, which implies that the positive commas smoothed the reading process around the target regions.

7 Conclusion

We proposed an approach for modeling comma placement in Chinese text for smoothing reading. In our approach, commas are added to the text on the basis of a CRF model-based comma predictor trained on the treebank, and a rule-based filter then classifies the commas into ones facilitating or obstructing reading. The experimental results on each part of this approach were encouraging.

In our future work, we would like see how commas affect reading by using much more material, and thereby refine our framework in order to bring a better reading experience to readers.

Acknowledgments

This research was partially supported by Kakenhi, MEXT Japan [23650076] and JST PRESTO.

References

Wallace Chafe. 1988. Punctuation and the prosody of written language. *Written Communication*, 5:396–426.

Yuqing Guo, Haifeng Wang, and Josef van Genabith. 2010. A linguistically inspired statistical model for Chinese punctuation generation. *ACM Transactions on Asian Language Information Processing*, 9(2):6:1–6:27, June.

Masako Hirotani, Lyn Frazier, and Keith Rayner. 2006. Punctuation and intonation effects on clause and sentence wrap-up: Evidence from eye movements. *Journal of Memory and Language*, 54(3):425–443.

Hen-Hsen Huang and Hsin-Hsi Chen. 2011. Pause and stop labeling for Chinese sentence boundary detection. In *Proceedings of Recent Advances in Natural Language Processing*, pages 146–153.

Jing Huang and Geoffrey Zweig. 2002. Maximum entropy model for punctuation annotation from speech. In *Proceedings of the International Conference on Spoken Language Processing*, pages 917–920.

Mei xun Jin, Mi-Young Kim, Dongil Kim, and Jong-Hyeok Lee. 2002. Segmentation of Chinese long sentences using commas. In *Proceedings of the Third SIGHAN Workshop on Chinese Language Processing*, pages 1–8.

John D. Lafferty, Andrew McCallum, and Fernando C. N. Pereira. 2001. Conditional random fields: Probabilistic models for segmenting and labeling sequence data. In *Proceedings of the Eighteenth International Conference on Machine Learning*, ICML '01, pages 282–289, San Francisco, CA, USA. Morgan Kaufmann Publishers Inc.

Robert Leaman and Graciela Gonzalez. 2008. BANNER: An executable survery of advances in biomedical named entity recognition. In *Pacific Symposium on Biocomputing (PSB'08)*, pages 652–663.

Baolin Liu, Zhongning Wang, and Zhixing Jin. 2010. The effects of punctuations in Chinese sentence comprehension: An erp study. *Journal of Neurolinguistics*, 23(1):66–68.

Wei Lu and Hwee Tou Ng. 2010. Better punctuation prediction with dynamic conditional random fields. In *Proceedings of the 2010 Conference on Empirical Methods in Natural Language Processing (EMNLP '10)*, pages 177–186.

Pascual Martínez-Gómez, Chen Chen, Tadayoshi Hara, Yoshinobu Kano, and Akiko Aizawa. 2012a. Image registration for text-gaze alignment. In *Proceedings of the 2012 ACM international conference on Intelligent User Interfaces (IUI '12)*, pages 257–260.

Pascual Martínez-Gómez, Tadayoshi Hara, Chen Chen, Kyohei Tomita, Yoshinobu Kano, and Akiko Aizawa. 2012b. Synthesizing image representations of linguistic and topological features for predicting areas of attention. In Patricia Anthony, Mitsuru Ishizuka, and Dickson Lukose, editors, *PRICAI 2012: Trends in Artificial Intelligence*, pages 312–323. Springer.

Andrew Kachites McCallum. 2002. MALLET: A machine learning for language toolkit.

Fu-dong Chiou Naiwen Xue, Fei Xia and Marta Palmer. 2005. The Penn Chinese TreeBank: Phrase structure annotation of a large corpus. *Natural Language Engineering*, 11(2):207–238.

Stephan Peitz, Markus Freitag, Arne Mauser, and Hermann Ney. 2011. Modeling punctuation prediction as machine translation. In *Proceedings of International Workshop on Spoken Language Translation*, pages 238–245.

Keith Rayner. 1998. Eye movements in reading and information processing: 20 years of research. *Psychological Bulletin*, 124(3):372–422.

Gui-Qin Ren and Yufang Yang. 2010. Syntactic boundaries and comma placement during silent reading of Chinese text: evidence from eye movements. *Journal of Research in Reading*, 33(2):168–177.

Burr Settles. 2005. ABNER: an open source tool for automatically tagging genes, proteins, and other entity names in text. *Bioinformatics*, 21(14):3191–3192.

Elizabeth Shriberg, Andreas Stolcke, Dilek Hakkani-Tür, and Gökhan Tür. 2000. Prosody-based automatic segmentation of speech into sentences and topics. *Speech Communication*, 32(1-2):127–154.

Judy Perkins Walker, Kirk Fongemie, and Tracy Daigle. 2001. Prosodic facilitation in the resolution of syntactic ambiguities in subjects with left and right hemisphere damage. *Brain and Language*, 78(2):169–196.

Nianwen Xue and Yaqin Yang. 2011. Chinese sentence segmentation as comma classification. In *Proceedings of the 49th Annual Meeting of the Association for Computational Linguistics:shortpapers*, pages 631–635.

Ming Yue. 2006. Discursive usage of six Chinese punctuation marks. In *Proceedings of the COLING/ACL 2006 Student Research Workshop*, pages 43–48.

ZDIC.NET. 2005. Commonly used Chinese punctuation usage short list. *Long Wiki*, Retrieved Dec 10, 2012, from http://www.zdic.net/appendix/f3.htm. (in Chinese).

X. Y. Zeng. 2006. The comparison and the use of English and Chinese comma. *College English*, 3(2):62–65. (in Chinese).

Kaixu Zhang, Yunqing Xia, and Hang Yu. 2006. CRF-based approach to sentence segmentation and punctuation for ancient Chinese prose. *Journal of Tsinghua Univ (Science and Technology)*, 49(10):1733–1736. (in Chinese).

On The Applicability of Readability Models to Web Texts

Sowmya Vajjala **Detmar Meurers**
Seminar für Sprachwissenschaft
Universität Tübingen
{sowmya,dm}@sfs.uni-tuebingen.de

Abstract

An increasing range of features is being used for automatic readability classification. The impact of the features typically is evaluated using reference corpora containing graded reading material. But how do the readability models and the features they are based on perform on real-world web texts? In this paper, we want to take a step towards understanding this aspect on the basis of a broad range of lexical and syntactic features and several web datasets we collected.

Applying our models to web search results, we find that the average reading level of the retrieved web documents is relatively high. At the same time, documents at a wide range of reading levels are identified and even among the Top-10 search results one finds documents at the lower levels, supporting the potential usefulness of readability ranking for the web. Finally, we report on generalization experiments showing that the features we used generalize well across different web sources.

1 Introduction

The web is a vast source of information on a broad range of topics. While modern search engines make use of a range of features for identifying and ranking search results, the question whether a web page presents its information in a form that is accessible to a given reader is only starting to receive attention. Researching the use of readability assessment as a ranking parameter for web search can be a relevant step in that direction.

Readability assessment has a long history spanning various fields of research from Educational Psychology to Computer Science. At the same time, the question which features generalize to different types of documents and whether the readability models are appropriate for real-life applications has only received little attention.

Against this backdrop, we want to see how well a state-of-the-art readability assessment approach using a broad range of features performs when applied to web data. Based on the approach introduced in Vajjala and Meurers (2012), we thus set out to explore the following two questions in this paper:

- Which reading levels can be identified in a systematic sample of web texts?
- How well do the features used generalize to different web sources?

The paper is organized as follows: Section 2 surveys related work. Section 3 introduces the corpus and the features we used. Section 4 describes our readability models. Section 5 discusses our experiments investigating the applicability of these models to web texts. Section 6 reports on a second set of experiments conducted to test the generalizability of the features used. Section 7 concludes the paper with a discussion of our results.

2 Related Work

2.1 Readability Assessment

The need for assessing the readability of a piece of text has been explored in the educational research community for over eight decades. DuBay (2006) provides an overview of early readability formulae, which were based on relatively shallow features and wordlists. Some of the formulae are still being used in practice, as exemplified by the Flesch-Kincaid Grade Level (Kincaid et al., 1975) available in Microsoft Word.

More recent computational linguistic approaches view readability assessment as a classification problem and explore different types of features. Statistical language modeling has been a popular approach (Si and Callan, 2001; Collins-Thompson and Callan, 2004), with the hypothesis that the word usage patterns across grade levels are distinctive enough. Heilman et. al. (2007; 2008) extended this approach by combining language models with manually and automatically extracted grammatical features.

The relation of text coherence and cohesion to readability is well explored in the CohMetrix project (McNamara et al., 2002). Ma et al. (2012a; 2012b) approached readability assessment as a ranking problem and also compared human versus automatic feature extraction for the task of labeling children's literature.

The WeeklyReader[1], an American educational newspaper with graded readers has been a popular source of data for readability classification research in the recent past. Petersen and Ostendorf (2009), Feng et al. (2009) and Feng (2010) used it to build readability models with a range of lexical, syntactic, language modeling and discourse features. In Vajjala and Meurers (2012) we created a larger corpus, *WeeBit*, by combining WeeklyReader with graded reading material from the BBCBitesize website.[2] We adapted measures of lexical richness and syntactic complexity from Second Language Acquisition (SLA) research as features for readability classification and showed that such measures of proficiency can successfully be used as features for readability assessment.

2.2 Readability Assessment of Web Texts

Despite the significant body of research on readability assessment, applying it to retrieve relevant texts from the web has elicited interest only in the recent past. While Bennöhr (2005) and Newbold et al. (2010) created new readability formulae for this purpose, Ott and Meurers (2010) and Tan et al. (2012) used existing readability formulae to filter search engine results. The READ-X project (Miltsakaki and Troutt, 2008; Miltsakaki, 2009) combined standard readability formulae with topic classification to retrieve relevant texts for users.

The REAP Project[3] supports the lexical acquisition of individual learners by retrieving texts that suit a given learner level. Kidwell et al. (2011) also used a word-acquisition model for readability prediction. Collins-Thompson et al. (2011) and Kim et al. (2012) employed word distribution based readability models for personalized search and for creating entity profiles respectively. Nakatani et al. (2010) followed a language modeling approach to rank search results to take user comprehension into account. Google also has an option to filter search results based on reading level, apparently using a language modeling approach.[4] Kanungo and Orr (2009) used search result snippet based features to predict the readability of short web-summaries.

All the above approaches primarily restrict themselves to traditional formulae or statistical language models encoding the distribution of words. The effect of lexical and syntactic features as used in recent research on readability thus remains to be studied in a web context. Furthermore, the generalizability of the features used to other data sets also remains to be explored. These are the primary issues we address in this paper.

3 Corpus and Features

Let us turn to answering our first question: Which reading levels can be identified in a systematic sample of web texts? To address this question, we first need to introduce the features we used, the graded corpus we used to train the model, and the nature of the readability model.

Since the goal of this paper is not to present new features but to explore the application of a readability approach to the web, we here simply adopt the feature and corpus setup introduced in Vajjala and Meurers (2012). The *WeeBit* corpus used is a corpus of texts belonging to five reading levels, corresponding to children of age group 7–16 years. It consists of 625 documents per reading level. The articles cover a range of fiction and nonfiction topics. Each article is labeled as belonging to one of five reading levels: Level 2, Level 3, Level 4, KS3 and GCSE.

We adapted both the lexical and syntactic features of Vajjala and Meurers (2012) to build readability models on the basis of the WeeBit corpus and then studied their applicability to real-world documents retrieved from the web as well as the applicability of those features across different web sources.

[1] `http://weeklyreader.com`

[2] `http://www.bbc.co.uk/bitesize`

[3] `http://reap.cs.cmu.edu`

[4] `http://goo.gl/aVy93`

Lexical features (LEXFEATURES) The lexical features are motivated by the lexical richness measures used to estimate the quality of language learners' oral narratives (Lu, 2012). We included several type-token ratio variants used in SLA research: generic type token ratio, root TTR, corrected TTR, bilogarithmic TTR and Uber Index.

In addition, there are lexical variation measures used to estimate the distribution of various parts of speech in the given text. They include the noun variation, adjective variation, modifier variation, adverb variation and verb variation, which represent the proportion of words of the respective part of speech categories compared to all lexical words in the document. Alternative measures for verb variation, namely, Squared Verb Variation and Corrected Verb Variation are also included. Apart from these, we also added the traditionally used measures of average number of characters per word, average number of syllables per word, and two readability formulae, the Flesch-Kincaid score (Kincaid et al., 1975) and the Coleman-Liau score (Coleman and Liau, 1975). Finally, we included the percentage of words from the Academic Word List[5]. It is a list created by Coxhead (2000) which consists of words that are more commonly found in academic texts.

Syntactic features (SYNFEATURES) These features are adapted from the syntactic complexity measures used to analyze second language writing (Lu, 2010). They are calculated based on the parser output of the BerkeleyParser (Petrov and Klein, 2007), using the Tregex (Levy and Andrew, 2006) pattern matcher. They include: mean lengths of various production units (sentence, clause and t-unit); clauses per sentence and t-unit; t-units per sentence; complex-t units per t-unit and per sentence; dependent clauses per clause, t-unit and sentence; co-ordinate phrases per clause, t-unit and sentence; complex nominals per clause and t-unit; noun phrases, verb phrases and preposition phrases per sentence; average length of NP, VP and PP; verb phrases per t-unit; SBARs per sentence and average parse tree height.

We refer to the feature subset containing all the traditionally used features (# char. per word, # syll. per word and # words per sentence) as TRADFEATURES in this paper.

[5]http://simple.wiktionary.org/wiki/Wiktionary:Academic_word_list

4 The Readability Model

In computational linguistics, readability assessment is generally approached as a classification problem. To our knowledge, only Heilman et al. (2008) and Ma et al. (2012a) experimented with other kinds of statistical models.

We approach readability assessment as a regression problem. This produces a model which provides a continuous estimate of the reading level, enabling us to see if there are documents that fall between two levels or above the maximal level found in the training data. We used the WEKA implementation of linear regression for this purpose. Since linear regression assumes that the data falls on an interval scale with evenly spaced reading levels, we used numeric values from 1–5 as reading levels instead of the original class names in the *WeeBit* corpus. Table 1 shows the mapping from WeeBit classes to numeric values, along with the age groups per class.

WeeBit class	Age (years)	Reading level
Level 2	7–8	1
Level 3	8–9	2
Level 4	9–10	3
KS3	11–14	4
GCSE	14–16	5

Table 1: *WeeBit* Reading Levels for Regression

We report Pearson's correlation coefficient and Root Mean Square Error (RMSE) as our evaluation metrics. Correlation coefficient measures the extent of linear relationship between two random variables. In readability assessment, a high correlation indicates that the texts at a higher difficulty level are more likely to receive a higher level prediction from the model and those at lower difficulty level would more likely receive a lower prediction. RMSE can be interpreted as the average deviation in grade levels between the predicted and the actual values.

We trained four regression models with the feature subsets introduced in section 3: LEXFEATURES, SYNFEATURES, TRADFEATURES and ALLFEATURES. While the criterion used in creating the graded texts in *WeeBit* is not known, it is likely that they were created with the traditional measures in mind. Indeed, the traditional features also were among the most predictive features in Vajjala and Meurers (2012). Hence, apart from training the above mentioned four regression models, we also trained a fifth model excluding the traditional features and formulae. This experiment was performed to verify if the traditional features are creating a skewed model that relies too heavily on those well-known and thus easily manipulated features in making decisions on test data. We refer to this fifth feature group as NoTrad.

Table 2 shows the result of our regression experiments using 10-fold cross-validation on the *WeeBit* corpus, employing the different feature subsets and the complete feature set.

Feature Set	# Features	Corr.	RMSE
LexFeatures	17	0.84	0.78
SynFeatures	25	0.88	0.64
TradFeatures	3	0.66	1.06
AllFeatures	42	**0.92**	**0.54**
NoTrad	37	0.89	0.63

Table 2: Linear Regression Results for *WeeBit*

The best correlation of 0.92 was achieved with the complete feature set. 0.92 is considered a strong correlation and coupled with an RMSE of 0.54, we can conclude that our regression model is a good model. In comparison, in Vajjala and Meurers (2012), where we tackle readability assessment as a classification problem, we obtained 93.3% accuracy on this dataset using all features.

Looking at the feature subsets, there also is a good correlation between the model predictions and the actual results in the other cases, except for the model considering only traditional features. While traditional features often are among the most predictive features in readability research, we also found that a model which does not include them can perform at a comparable level (0.89).

Comparing these results with previous research using regression modeling for readability assessment is not particularly meaningful because of the differences in the corpus and the levels used. For example, while Heilman et al. (2008) used a corpus of 289 texts across 12 reading levels achieving a correlation of 0.77, we used the *WeeBit* corpus containing 3125 texts across 5 reading levels.[6]

We took the two best models of Table 2, ModAll using AllFeatures and ModNoTrad using the NoTrad feature set, and set out to answer our first guiding question, about the reading levels which such models can identify in a systematic sample of web texts.

5 Applying readability models to web texts

To investigate the effect of the two readability models for real-world web texts, we studied their performance on two types of web data:

- web documents we crawled from specific web sites that offer the same type of material for two groups of readers differing in their reading skills
- web documents identified by a web search engine for a sample of web queries selected from a public query log

5.1 Readability of web data drawn from characteristic web sites

5.1.1 Web test sets used

Following the approach of Collins-Thompson and Callan (2005) and Sato et al. (2008), who evaluated readability models using independent web-based test sets, we compiled three sets of web documents that given their origin can be classified into two classes each:

Wiki – SimpleWiki: Wikipedia[7], along with its manually simplified version *Simple Wikipedia*[8] is increasingly used in two-class readability classification tasks and text simplification approaches (Napoles and Dredze, 2010; Zhu et al., 2010; Coster and Kauchak, 2011). We use a collection of 2000 randomly selected parallel articles from each of the two websites, which in the following is referred to as Wiki and SimpleWiki.

Time – Time for Kids: *Time for Kids*[9] is a division of the TIME magazine[10], which produces articles exclusively for children and is used widely in classrooms. We took a sample of 2000 documents each from Time and from Time for Kids for our experiments and refer them Time and TfK.

NormalNews – ChildrensNews: We crawled websites that contain news articles written for children (e.g., `http://www.firstnews.co.uk`) and categorized them as ChildrensNews. We also crawled freely accessible articles from popular news websites such as *BBC* or *The Guardian* and

[6]Direct comparisons on the same data set would be most indicative, but many datasets, such as the corpus used in Heilman et al. (2008), are not accessible due to copyright issues.

[7]`http://en.wikipedia.org`
[8]`http://simple.wikipedia.org`
[9]`http://www.timeforkids.com`
[10]`http://www.time.com`

categorized them as NORMALNEWS. We took 10K documents from each of these two categories for our experiments.

These three corpus pairs collected as test cases differ in several aspects. For example, SimpleWikipedia is not targeting children as such, whereas Time for Kids and ChildrensNews are. And SimpleWikipedia – Wikipedia covers parallel articles in two versions, whereas this is not the case for the the two Time and the two News corpora. However, as far as we see these differences are orthogonal to the issue we are researching here, namely their use as real-life test cases to study the effect of the classification model learned on the WeeBit data.

We applied the two regression models which had performed best on the *WeeBit* corpus (cf. Table 2 in section 4) to these web datasets. The average reading levels of the different datasets according to these two models are reported in Table 3.

Data Set	MODALL	MODNOTRAD
SIMPLEWIKI	3.86	2.67
TFK	4.15	2.72
CHILDRENSNEWS	4.19	2.39
WIKI	4.21	3.33
TIME	5.04	4.07
NORMALNEWS	5.58	4.42

Table 3: Applying the *WeeBit* regression model to the six web datasets

The table shows that both MODALL and MODNOTRAD place the documents from the children websites (SIMPLEWIKI, TFK and CHILDRENSNEWS) at lower reading levels than those from the regular websites for adults (TIME, WIKI and NORMALNEWS). However, there is an interesting difference in the predictions made by the two models. The MODALL model including the traditional features consistently assigns a higher reading level to all the documents, and it also fails to separate CHILDRENSNEWS (4.19) from WIKI (4.20).

To be able to inspect this in detail, we plotted the class-wise reading level distribution of our regression models. Figure 1 shows the distribution of reading levels for these web datasets using MODALL. As we already knew from the averages, the model assigns somewhat higher reading levels to all documents, and the figure confirms that the texts for children (SIMPLEWIKI, TFK and CHILDRENSNEWS) are only marginally distinguished from the corresponding websites targeting adult readers (TIME,WIKI and NORMALNEWS). The NORMALNEWS dataset also seems to be placed in a much higher distribution compared to all the other test sets, with more than 50% of the documents getting a prediction of "higher" (the label used for documents placed at level 6 or higher).

Figure 2 shows the distribution of reading levels across the test sets according to MODNOTRAD, the model without traditional features. The model provides a broader coverage across all reading levels, with documents from children web sites and SimpleWikipedia clearly being placed at the lower end of the spectrum and web pages targeting adults at the higher end. NORMALNEWS documents are again placed the highest, but less than 10% fall outside the range established by WeeBit. TIME shows the highest diversity, with around 20% for each reading level above the lowest one.

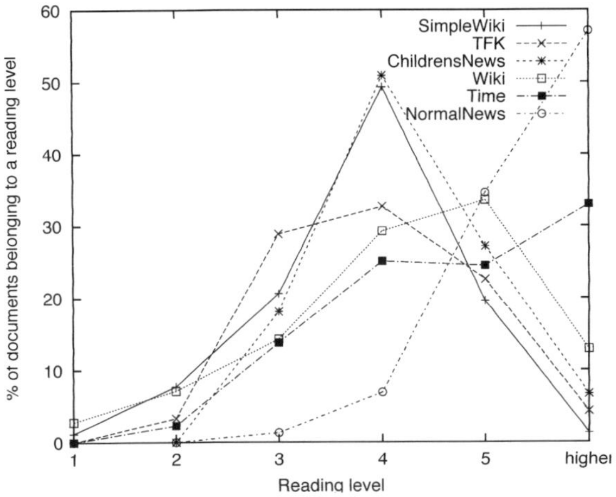

Figure 1: Reading levels assigned by MODALL

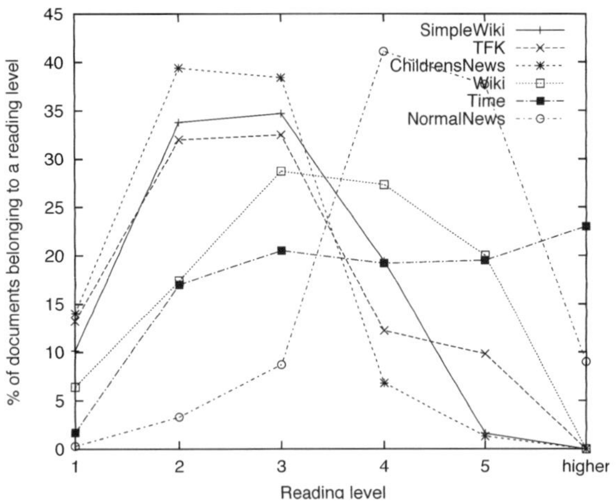

Figure 2: Reading levels using MODNOTRAD

The first set of experiments shows that the readability models which were successful on the *WeeBit* reference corpus seem to be able to identify a corresponding broad range among web documents that we selected top-down by relying on prototypical websites targeting "adult" and "child" readers, which are likely to feature more difficult and easier web documents, respectively. While we cannot evaluate the difference between the two models quantitatively, given the lack of an external gold standard classification of the crawled data, the MODNOTRAD conceptually seems to do a better job at distinguishing the two classes of websites in line with the top-down expectations.

5.2 Readability of search results

Complementing the first set of experiments, establishing that the readability models are capable of placing web documents in line with the top-down classification of the sites they originate from, in the second set of experiments we want to investigate bottom-up whether for some random topics of interest, the web offers texts at different readability levels. This also is of practical relevance, since ranking web search results by readability is only useful if there actually are documents at different reading levels for a given query.

For this investigation, we took the MODNOTRAD model and used it to estimate the reading level of web search results. For web searching, we used the BING search API (`http://datamarket.azure.com/dataset/bing/search`) and computed the reading levels of the Top-100 search results for a sample of 50 test queries, selected from a publicly accessible database (Lu and Callan, 2003).

Figure 3 characterizes the data obtained through the web searches in terms of the percentage of documents belonging to a given reading level, according to the MODNOTRAD model. In the Top-100 search results obtained for each of the 50 queries, the model identifies documents at all reading levels, with a peak at reading level 4 (corresponding to KS3 in the original WeeBit dataset).

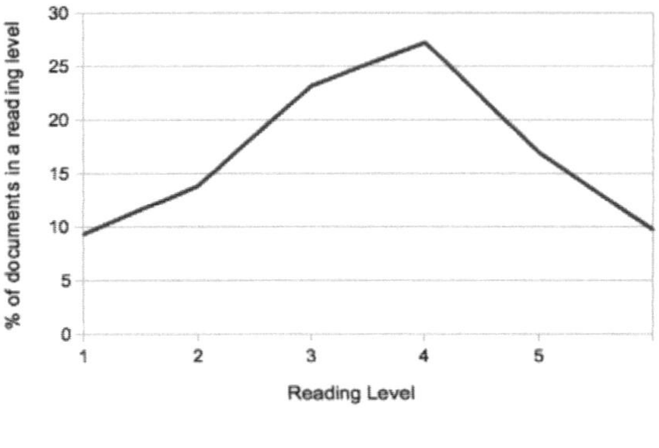

Figure 3: Documents retrieved per reading level

To determine how much individual queries differ in terms of the readability of the documents they retrieve, we also looked at the results for each query separately. Figure 4 shows the mean reading level of the Top-100 results for each of the 50 search queries. From query to query, the average readability of the documents retrieved seems to differ relatively little, with most results falling into the higher reading levels (4 or above).

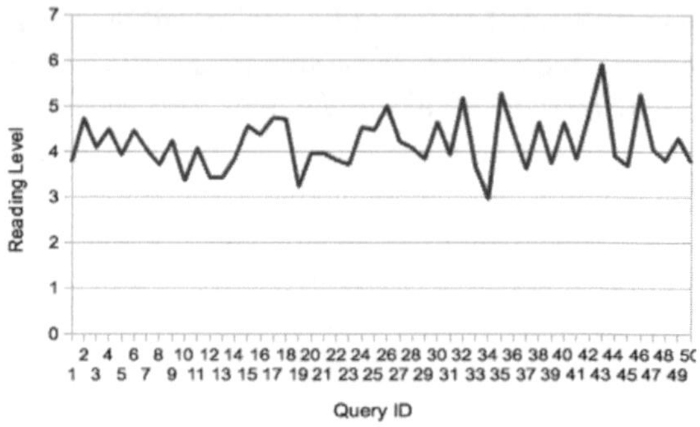

Figure 4: Average reading level of search results

Returning to the question whether there are documents of different reading levels for a given query, we need to check how much variation exists around the observed, rather similar averages. Table 4 provides the individual reading levels of the Top-10 search results for a sample of 10 queries from our experiment, along with the average reading level of the Top-100 results for that query. The results in Table 4 indicate that indeed there are documents at a broad range of reading levels even among the most relevant search results returned by the BING web search engine.

Looking at the individual query results, we found that although a lot of news documents tended towards a higher reading level, it is indeed possible to find some texts at lower reading levels even within Top-10 results (indicated in bold). However, we found that even for queries that we would expect to result in hits from websites targeting child readers, those sites often did not make it into the Top-10 results. The same was true for sites offering "simple" language, such as Simple Wikipedia, which was not among the top

Result Rank →	1	2	3	4	5	6	7	8	9	10	Avg_{Top100}
Query											
local anaesthetic	3.18	4.57	5.35	3.09	4.24	4.6	3.95	4.74	**2.72**	4.73	3.78
copyright copy law	1.77	4.59	1.43	2.67	4.63	6.2	2.69	**1.1**	3.87	5.61	4.57
halley comet	**1.69**	4.47	4.54	4.24	2.37	4.1	4.86	3.56	4.21	3.56	4.04
public offer	4.4	4.35	5.06	5.03	4.36	5.16	4.13	4.67	3.81	**1.1**	4.39
optic sensor	2.67	3.38	4.5	3.17	2.54	4.19	4.84	**1.47**	2.2	3.31	3.83
europe union politics	3.61	4.9	6.3	4.02	2.17	4.5	**1.47**	1.58	4.88	6.33	4.33
presidential poll	4.98	5.38	1.77	6.1	4.76	3.82	**1.05**	5.11	3.92	4.25	3.95
shakespeare	2.39	2.9	4.2	4.74	4.76	3.89	**1.47**	2.13	2.6	4.06	3.58
air pollution	**1.17**	4.93	3.7	2.3	4.36	3.73	3.71	3.49	2.22	2.67	4.21
euclidean geometry	3.88	4.71	4.7	4.3	4.45	4.63	4.04	4.1	3.48	**2.58**	3.18

Table 4: Reading levels of individual search results

results even when it contained pages directly relevant to the query. To provide access to those pages, reranking the search results based on readability would thus be of value.

While we do not want to jump to conclusions based on our sample of 50 queries, the results of our experiments seem to support the idea that readability-based re-ranking of web search results can help users in accessing web documents that also are at the right level for the given user. Returning to the first overall question that lead us here, our experiments support the answer that indeed there are documents spread across different reading levels on the web with a tendency towards higher reading levels.

6 Generalizability of the Feature Set

We can now turn to the second question raised in the introduction: How well do the features generalize across different classes of web documents? We saw in section 5.1 that the predictions of the two models we used varied quite a bit, solely based on whether the traditional readability features were included in the model or not. This confirms the need to investigate how generally applicable which types of features are across datasets.

As far as we know, such an experiment validating the generalizability of features was not yet performed in this domain. As there are no publicly available graded web datasets to build new readability models with the same feature set, we used the datasets we introduced in section 5.1.1 for creating two-class readability classification models. Since there are no clear age-group annotations with all these datasets, we decided to use a broad two-level classification instead of more fine grained grade levels.

The difference between this experiment and the previous one lies in the primary question it attempts to answer. Here, the focus is on verifying if the features are capable of building accurate classification models on different training sets. In the previous experiment, it was on checking if a given classification model (which in that experiment was trained on the WeeBit corpus) can successfully discriminate reading levels for documents from various real-world texts.

We observed in Section 5.1 that with traditional features, the WeeBit based readability model assigned higher reading levels to all the documents from our web datasets. So, it would perhaps be a natural step to train these binary classification models excluding the traditional features. However, the traditional features may still be useful (with different weights) for constructing classification models with other training data. So, we trained two sets of models per training set – one with ALLFEATURES and another excluding traditional features (NOTRAD).

We trained binary classification models using the following training sets:

- TIME – TFK texts
- WIKI – SIMPLEWIKI texts
- NORMALNEWS – KIDSNEWS texts
- TIME+WIKI – TFK+SIMPLEWIKI texts

We used the Sequential Minimal Optimization (SMO) algorithm implementation in the WEKA tool kit to train these classifiers. The choice of the algorithm here was motivated by the fact that training is quick and that SMO has successfully been used in previous research on readability assessment (Feng, 2010; Hancke et al., 2012).

Table 5 summarizes the classification accuracies obtained with the four models using 10-fold cross validation for the four web corpora.

Training Set	Accuracy-All	Accuracy-NoTrad
TIME – TFK	95.11%	89.52%
WIKI – SIMPLEWIKI	92.32%	88.81%
NORMALNEWS – KIDSNEWS	97.93%	92.54%
TIME+WIKI – TFK+SIMPLEWIKI	93.38%	89.72%

Table 5: Cross-validation accuracies for binary classification on different web corpora

The results in the table show that the same set of features consistently result in creating accurate classification models for all four web corpora. Each of the two-class classification models performed well, despite the fact that the documents were created by different people and most likely with different instructions on how to write simple texts or simplify already existing texts. It was interesting to note the role of traditional features in improving the accuracy of these binary classification models. But, in the previous experiment, the model with traditional features consistently put all the documents into higher reading levels. It is possible that the role of traditional features in the WeeBit corpus may be skewed as it is likely that it was prepared with traditional readability measures in mind. Contrasting the results of these two experiments raises the question of what features hold more weight in what dataset, which is an interesting issue to explore in the future.

In sum, this experiment provides some clear evidence for affirmatively answering the second question about the generalizability of the feature set we used. The features seem to be sufficiently general for them to be useful in performing readability assessment of real-world documents.

7 Conclusion and Discussion

In this paper, we set out to investigate the applicability and generalizability of readability models for real-world web texts. We started with building readability models using linear regression, on a 5-level readability corpus with a range of lexical and syntactic features (section 4). We applied the two best models thus obtained to several web datasets we compiled from websites targeting children and others designed for adults (section 5.1) and on the Top-100 results obtained using a standard web search engine (section 5.2).

We observed that the models identified texts across a broad range of reading levels in the web corpora. Our pilot study of the reading levels of the search results confirmed that readability models could be useful as re-ranking or filtering parameters that prioritize relevant results which are at the right level for a given user. At the same time, we observed in both these experiments that the average reading level of general web articles is relatively high according to our models. Apart from result ranking, this also calls for the construction of efficient text simplification systems which pick up the difficult texts and attempt to simplify them to a given reading level.

We then proceeded to investigate how well the features used to build these readability models generalize across different corpora. For this, we reused the corpora with articles for children and adult readers from prototypical websites (section 5.1.1) and built four binary classification models with all of the readability features (section 6). Each of the models achieved good classification accuracies, supporting that the broad feature set used generalizes well across corpora. Whether or not to use traditional readability features is somewhat difficult to answer since those formulae are often taken into account when writing materials, so high classification accuracy on such corpora may be superficial in that it is not necessarily indicative of the spectrum of texts found on the web (section 5.1). This also raises the more general question which features work best for which kind of dataset. A systematic exploration of the effect of the individual features along with the impact of document topic and genre on readability would be interesting and relevant to pursue in the future.

In our future work, we also intend to explore further features for this task and improve our understanding of the correlations between the different features. Finally, we are considering reformulating readability assessment as ordinal regression or preference ranking.

Acknowledgements

We would like to thank the anonymous reviewers for their detailed, useful comments on the paper. This research was funded by the European Commission's 7th Framework Program under grant agreement number 238405 (CLARA).

References

Jasmine Bennöhr. 2005. A web-based personalised textfinder for language learners. Master's thesis, School of Informatics, University of Edinburgh.

Meri Coleman and T. L. Liau. 1975. A computer readability formula designed for machine scoring. *Journal of Applied Psychology*, 60:283–284.

Kevyn Collins-Thompson and Jamie Callan. 2004. A language modeling approach to predicting reading difficulty. In *Proceedings of HLT/NAACL 2004*, Boston, USA.

Kevyn Collins-Thompson and Jamie Callan. 2005. Predicting reading difficulty with statistical language models. *Journal of the American Society for Information Science and Technology*, 56(13):1448–1462.

K. Collins-Thompson, P. N. Bennett, R. W. White, S. de la Chica, and D. Sontag. 2011. Personalizing web search results by reading level. In *Proceedings of the Twentieth ACM International Conference on Information and Knowledge Management (CIKM 2011)*.

William Coster and David Kauchak. 2011. Simple english wikipedia: A new text simplification task. In *Proceedings of the 49th Annual Meeting of the Association for Computational Linguistics: Human Language Technologies*, pages 665–669, Portland, Oregon, USA, June. Association for Computational Linguistics.

Averil Coxhead. 2000. A new academic word list. *Teachers of English to Speakers of Other Languages*, 34(2):213–238.

William H. DuBay. 2006. *The Classic Readability Studies*. Impact Information, Costa Mesa, California.

Lijun Feng, Nomie Elhadad, and Matt Huenerfauth. 2009. Cognitively motivated features for readability assessment. In *Proceedings of the 12th Conference of the European Chapter of the ACL (EACL 2009)*, pages 229–237, Athens, Greece, March. Association for Computational Linguistics.

Lijun Feng. 2010. *Automatic Readability Assessment*. Ph.D. thesis, City University of New York (CUNY).

Julia Hancke, Detmar Meurers, and Sowmya Vajjala. 2012. Readability classification for german using lexical, syntactic, and morphological features. In *Proceedings of the 24th International Conference on Computational Linguistics (COLING)*, pages 1063–1080, Mumbay, India.

Michael Heilman, Kevyn Collins-Thompson, Jamie Callan, and Maxine Eskenazi. 2007. Combining lexical and grammatical features to improve readability measures for first and second language texts. In *Human Language Technologies 2007: The Conference of the North American Chapter of the Association for Computational Linguistics (HLT-NAACL-07)*, pages 460–467, Rochester, New York.

Michael Heilman, Kevyn Collins-Thompson, and Maxine Eskenazi. 2008. An analysis of statistical models and features for reading difficulty prediction. In *Proceedings of the 3rd Workshop on Innovative Use of NLP for Building Educational Applications at ACL-08*, Columbus, Ohio.

Tapas Kanungo and David Orr. 2009. Predicting the readability of short web summaries. In *Proceedings of the Second ACM International Conference on Web Search and Data Mining*, WSDM '09, pages 202–211, New York, NY, USA. ACM.

P. Kidwell, G. Lebanon, and K. Collins-Thompson. 2011. Statistical estimation of word acquisition with application to readability prediction. In *Journal of the American Statistical Association. 106(493):21-30.*

Jin Young Kim, Kevyn Collins-Thompson, Paul N. Bennett, and Susan T. Dumais. 2012. Characterizing web content, user interests, and search behavior by reading level and topic. In *Proceedings of the fifth ACM international conference on Web search and data mining*, WSDM '12, pages 213–222, New York, NY, USA. ACM.

J. P. Kincaid, R. P. Jr. Fishburne, R. L. Rogers, and B. S Chissom. 1975. Derivation of new readability formulas (Automated Readability Index, Fog Count and Flesch Reading Ease formula) for Navy enlisted personnel. Research Branch Report 8-75, Naval Technical Training Command, Millington, TN.

Roger Levy and Galen Andrew. 2006. Tregex and tsurgeon: tools for querying and manipulating tree data structures. In *5th International Conference on Language Resources and Evaluation*, Genoa, Italy.

Jie Lu and Jamie Callan. 2003. Content-based retrieval in hybrid peer-to-peer networks. In *Proceedings of the Twelfth International Conference on Information and Knowledge Management (CIKM'03)*.

Xiaofei Lu. 2010. Automatic analysis of syntactic complexity in second language writing. *International Journal of Corpus Linguistics*, 15(4):474–496.

Xiaofei Lu. 2012. The relationship of lexical richness to the quality of ESL learners' oral narratives. *The Modern Languages Journal*, pages 190–208.

Yi Ma, Eric Fosler-Lussier, and Robert Lofthus. 2012a. Ranking-based readability assessment for early primary children's literature. In *Proceedings of the 2012 Conference of the North American Chapter of the Association for Computational Linguistics: Human Language Technologies*, NAACL HLT '12, pages 548–552, Stroudsburg, PA, USA. Association for Computational Linguistics.

Yi Ma, Ritu Singh, Eric Fosler-Lussier, and Robert Lofthus. 2012b. Comparing human versus automatic feature extraction for fine-grained elementary readability assessment. In *Proceedings of the First Workshop on Predicting and Improving Text Readability for target reader populations*, PITR '12, pages 58–64, Stroudsburg, PA, USA. Association for Computational Linguistics.

Danielle S. McNamara, Max M. Louwerse, and Arthur C. Graesser. 2002. Coh-metrix: Automated cohesion and coherence scores to predict text readability and facilitate comprehension. Proposal of Project funded by the Office of Educational Research and Improvement, Reading Program.

Eleni Miltsakaki and Audrey Troutt. 2008. Real time web text classification and analysis of reading difficulty. In *Proceedings of the Third Workshop on Innovative Use of NLP for Building Educational Applications (BEA-3) at ACL'08*, pages 89–97, Columbus, Ohio. Association for Computational Linguistics.

Eleni Miltsakaki. 2009. Matching readers' preferences and reading skills with appropriate web texts. In *Proceedings of the 12th Conference of the European Chapter of the Association for Computational Linguistics: Demonstrations Session*, EACL '09, pages 49–52, Stroudsburg, PA, USA. Association for Computational Linguistics.

Makoto Nakatani, Adam Jatowt, and Katsumi Tanaka. 2010. Adaptive ranking of search results by considering user's comprehension. In *Proceedings of the 4th International Conference on Ubiquitous Information Management and Communication (ICUIMC 2010)*, pages 182–192. ACM Press, Suwon, Korea.

Courtney Napoles and Mark Dredze. 2010. Learning simple wikipedia: a cogitation in ascertaining abecedarian language. In *Proceedings of the NAACL HLT 2010 Workshop on Computational Linguistics and Writing: Writing Processes and Authoring Aids*, CL&W '10, pages 42–50, Stroudsburg, PA, USA. Association for Computational Linguistics.

Neil Newbold, Harry McLaughlin, and Lee Gillam. 2010. Rank by readability: Document weighting for information retrieval. In Hamish Cunningham, Allan Hanbury, and Stefan Rüger, editors, *Advances in Multidisciplinary Retrieval*, volume 6107 of *Lecture Notes in Computer Science*, pages 20–30. Springer Berlin / Heidelberg.

Niels Ott and Detmar Meurers. 2010. Information retrieval for education: Making search engines language aware. *Themes in Science and Technology Education. Special issue on computer-aided language analysis, teaching and learning: Approaches, perspectives and applications*, 3(1–2):9–30.

Sarah E. Petersen and Mari Ostendorf. 2009. A machine learning approach to reading level assessment. *Computer Speech and Language*, 23:86–106.

Slav Petrov and Dan Klein. 2007. Improved inference for unlexicalized parsing. In *Human Language Technologies 2007: The Conference of the North American Chapter of the Association for Computational Linguistics; Proceedings of the Main Conference*, pages 404–411, Rochester, New York, April.

Satoshi Sato, Suguru Matsuyoshi, and Yohsuke Kondoh. 2008. Automatic assessment of japanese text readability based on a textbook corpus. In *LREC'08*.

Luo Si and Jamie Callan. 2001. A statistical model for scientific readability. In *Proceedings of the 10th International Conference on Information and Knowledge Management (CIKM)*, pages 574–576. ACM.

Chenhao Tan, Evgeniy Gabrilovich, and Bo Pang. 2012. To each his own: Personalized content selection based on text comprehensibility. In *In Proceedings of WSDM*.

Sowmya Vajjala and Detmar Meurers. 2012. On improving the accuracy of readability classification using insights from second language acquisition. In Joel Tetreault, Jill Burstein, and Claudial Leacock, editors, *Proceedings of the 7th Workshop on Innovative Use of NLP for Building Educational Applications (BEA7) at NAACL-HLT*, pages 163–173, Montral, Canada, June. Association for Computational Linguistics.

Zhemin Zhu, Delphine Bernhard, and Iryna Gurevych. 2010. A monolingual tree-based translation model for sentence simplification. In *Proceedings of The 23rd International Conference on Computational Linguistics (COLING), August 2010. Beijing, China.*

The CW Corpus: A New Resource for Evaluating the Identification of Complex Words

Matthew Shardlow
Text Mining Research Group
School of Computer Science, University of Manchester
IT301, Kilburn Building, Manchester, M13 9PL, England
m.shardlow@cs.man.ac.uk

Abstract

The task of identifying complex words (CWs) is important for lexical simplification, however it is often carried out with no evaluation of success. There is no basis for comparison of current techniques and, prior to this work, there has been no standard corpus or evaluation technique for the CW identification task. This paper addresses these shortcomings with a new corpus for evaluating a system's performance in identifying CWs. Simple Wikipedia edit histories were mined for instances of single word lexical simplifications. The corpus contains 731 sentences, each with one annotated CW. This paper describes the method used to produce the CW corpus and presents the results of evaluation, showing its validity.

1 Introduction

CW identification techniques are typically implemented as a preliminary step in a lexical simplification system. The evaluation of the identification of CWs is an often forgotten task. Omitting this can cause a loss of accuracy at this stage which will adversely affect the following processes and hence the user's understanding of the resulting text.

Previous approaches to the CW identification task (see Section 5) have generally omitted an evaluation of their method. This gap in the literature highlights the need for evaluation, for which gold standard data is needed. This research proposes the CW corpus, a dataset of 731 examples of sentences with exactly one annotated CW per sentence.

A CW is defined as one which causes a sentence to be more difficult for a user to read. For example, in the following sentence:

'The cat reposed on the mat'

The presence of the word 'reposed' would reduce the understandability for some readers. It would be difficult for some readers to work out the sentence's meaning, and if the reader is unfamiliar with the word 'reposed', they will have to infer its meaning from the surrounding context. Replacing this word with a more familiar alternative, such as 'sat', improves the understandability of the sentence, whilst retaining the majority of the original semantics.

Retention of meaning is an important factor during lexical simplification. If the word 'reposed' is changed to 'sat', then the specific meaning of the sentence will be modified (generally speaking, reposed may indicate a state of relaxation, whereas sat indicates a body position) although the broad meaning is still the same (a cat is on a mat in both scenarios). Semantic shift should be kept to a minimum during lexical simplification. Recent work (Biran et al., 2011; Bott et al., 2012) has employed distributional semantics to ensure simplifications are of sufficient semantic similarity.

Word complexity is affected by many factors such as familiarity, context, morphology and length. Furthermore, these factors change from person to person and context to context. The same word, in a different sentence, may be perceived as being of a different level of difficulty. The same word in the same sentence, but read by a different person, may also be perceived as different in difficulty. For example, a person who speaks English as a second language will struggle with unfamiliar words depending on their native tongue. Conversely, the reader who has a low reading ability will struggle with long and obscure words. Whilst there will be some crossover in the language these two groups find difficult, this will not be exactly the same. This subjectivity makes the automation and evaluation of CW identification difficult.

Subjectivity makes the task of natural language generation difficult and rules out automatically generating annotated complex sentences. Instead, our CW discovery process (presented in Section 2) mines simplifications from Simple Wikipedia[1] edit histories. Simple Wikipedia is well suited to this task as it is a website where language is collaboratively and iteratively simplified by a team of editors. These editors follow a set of strict guidelines and accountability is enforced by the self policing community. Simple Wikipedia is aimed at readers with a low English reading ability such as children or people with English as a second language. The type of simplifications found in Wikipedia and thus mined for use in our corpus are therefore appropriate for people with low English proficiency. By capturing these simplifications, we produce a set of genuine examples of sentences which can be used to evaluate the performance of CW identification systems. It should be noted that although these simplifications are best suited to low English proficiency users, the CW identification techniques that will be evaluated using the corpus can be trained and applied for a variety of user groups.

The contributions of this paper are as follows:

- A description of the method used to create the CW corpus. Section 2.
- An analysis of the corpus combining results from 6 human annotators. Section 3.
- A discussion on the practicalities surrounding the use of the CW corpus for the evaluation of a CW identification system. Section 4.

Related and future work are also presented in Sections 5 and 6 respectively.

2 Design

Our corpus contains examples of simplifications which have been made by human editors during their revisions of Simple Wikipedia articles. These are in the form of sentences with one word which has been identified as requiring simplification.[2] These examples can be used to evaluate the output of a CW identification system (see Section 6). To make the discovery and evaluation task easier, we limit the discovered simplifications to one word per sentence. So, if an edited sentence differs from its original by more than one word, we do not include it in our corpus. This also promotes uniformity in the corpus, reducing the complexity of the evaluation task.

System	Score
SUBTLEX	0.3352
Wikipedia Baseline	0.3270
Kučera-Francis	0.3097
Random Baseline	0.0157

Table 1: The results of different experiments on the SemEval lexical simplification data (de Belder and Moens, 2012), showing the SUBTLEX data's superior performance over several baselines. Each baseline gave a familiarity value to a set of words based on their frequency of occurrence. These values were used to produce a ranking over the data which was compared with a gold standard ranking using kappa agreement to give the scores shown here. A baseline using the Google Web 1T dataset was shown to give a higher score than SUBTLEX, however this dataset was not available during the course of this research.

2.1 Preliminaries

SUBTLEX

The SUBTLEX dataset (Brysbaert and New, 2009) is used as a familiarity dictionary. Its primary function is to associate words with their frequencies of occurrence, assuming that words which occur more frequently are simpler. SUBTLEX is also used as a dictionary for testing word existence: if a word does not occur in the dataset, it is not considered for simplification. This may occur in the case of very infrequent words or proper nouns. The

[1] http://simple.wikipedia.org/

[2] We also record the simplification suggested by the original Simple Wikipedia editor.

SUBTLEX data is chosen over the more conventional Kučera-Francis frequency (Kučera and Francis, 1967) and over a baseline produced from Wikipedia frequencies due to a previous experiment using a lexical simplification dataset from task 1 of SemEval 2012 (de Belder and Moens, 2012). See Table 1.

Word Sense

Homonymy is the phenomenon of a wordform having 2 distinct meanings as in the classic case: '*Bank* of England' vs. 'River *bank*'. In each case, the word *bank* is referring to a different semantic entity. This presents a problem when calculating word frequency as the frequencies for homonyms will be combined. Word sense disambiguation is an unsolved problem and was not addressed whilst creating the CW corpus. The role of word sense in lexical simplification will be investigated at a later stage of this research.

Yatskar et al. (2010)

The CW corpus was built following the work of Yatskar et al. (2010) in identifying paraphrases from Simple Wikipedia edit histories. Their method extracts lexical edits from aligned sentences in adjacent revisions of a Simple Wikipedia article. These lexical edits are then processed to determine their likelihood of being a true simplification. Two methods for determining this probability are presented, the first uses conditional probability to determine whether a lexical edit represents a simplification and the second uses metadata from comments to generate a set of trusted revisions, from which simplifications can be detected using pointwise mutual information. Our method (further explained in Section 2.2) differs from their work in several ways. Firstly, we seek to discover only single word lexical edits. Secondly, we use both article metadata and a series of strict checks against a lexicon, a thesaurus and a simplification dictionary to ensure that the extracted lexical edits are true simplifications. Thirdly, we retain the original context of the simplification as lexical complexity is thought to be influenced by context (Biran et al., 2011; Bott et al., 2012).

Automatically mining edit histories was chosen as it provides many instances quickly and at a low cost. The other method of creating a similar corpus would have been to ask several professionally trained annotators to produce hundreds of sets of sentences, and to mark up the CWs in these. The use of professionals would be expensive and annotators may not agree on the way in which words should be simplified, leading to further problems when combining annotations.

2.2 Method

In this section, we explain the procedure to create the corpus. There are many processing stages as represented graphically in Figure 1. The stages in the diagram are further described in the sections below. For simplicity, we view Simple Wikipedia as a set of pages P, each with an associated set of revisions R. Every revision of every page is processed iteratively until P is exhausted.

Content Articles

The Simple Wikipedia edit histories were obtained.[3] The entire database was very large, so only main content articles were considered. All user, talk and meta articles were discarded. Non-content articles are not intended to be read by typical users and so may not reflect the same level of simplicity as the rest of the site.

Revisions which Simplify

When editing a Simple Wikipedia article, the author has the option to attach a comment to their revision. Following the work of Yatskar et al. (2010), we only consider those revisions which have a comment containing some morphological equivalent of the lemma 'simple', e.g. simplify, simplifies, simplification, simpler, etc. This allows us to search for comments where the author states that they are simplifying the article.

Tf-idf Matrix

Each revision is a set of sentences. As changes from revision to revision are often small, there will be many sentences which are the same in adjacent revisions. Sentences which are likely to contain a simplification will only have one word difference and sentences which are unrelated will have many different words. Tf-idf (Salton and Yang, 1973) vectors are calculated

[3]Database dump dated 4th February 2012.

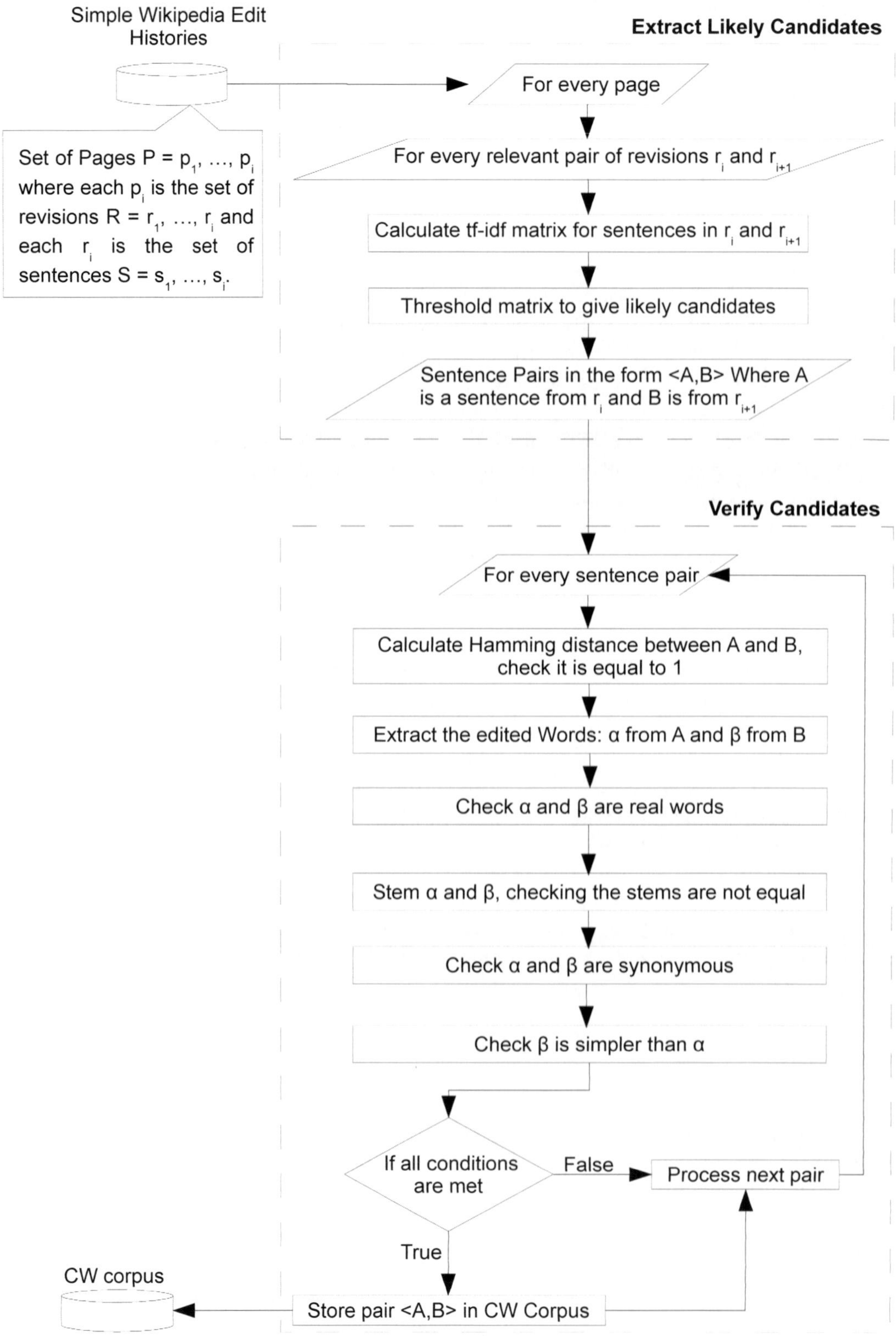

Figure 1: A flow chart showing the process undertaken to extract lexical simplifications. Each part of this process is further explained in Section 2.2. Every pair of revisions from every relevant page is processed, although the appropriate recursion is omitted from the flow chart for simplicity.

for each sentence and the matrix containing the dot product of every pair of sentence vectors from the first and second revision is calculated. This allows us to easily see those vectors which are exactly the same — as these will have a score of one.[4] It also allows us to easily see which vectors are so different that they could not contain a one word edit. We empirically set a threshold at $0.9 <= X < 1$ to capture those sentences which were highly related, but not exactly the same.

Candidate Pairs

The above process resulted in pairs of sentences which were very similar according to the tf-idf metric. These pairs were then subjected to a series of checks as detailed below. These were designed to ensure that as few false positives as possible would make it to the corpus. This may have meant discarding some true positives too, however the cautious approach was adopted to ensure a higher corpus accuracy.

Hamming Distance

We are only interested in those sentences with a difference of one word, because sentences with more than one word difference may contain several simplifications or may be a rewording. It is more difficult to distinguish whether these are true simplifications. We calculate the Hamming distance between sentences (using wordforms as base units) to ensure that only one word differs. Any sentence pairs which do not have a Hamming distance of 1 are discarded.

Reality Check

The first check is to ensure that both the words are a part of our lexicon, ensuring that there is SUBTLEX frequency data for these words and also that they are valid words. This stage may involve removing some valid words, which are not found in the lexicon, however this is preferable to allowing words that are the result of spam or vandalism.

[4] As tf-idf treats a sentence as a bag of words it is possible for two sentences to give a score of 1 if they contain the same words, but in a different order. This is not a problem as if the sentence order is different, there is a minimum of 2 lexical edits — meaning we still wish to discount this pair.

Inequality Check

It is possible that although a different word is present, it is a morphological variant of the original word rather than a simplification. E.g., due to a change in tense, or a correction. To identify this, we stem both words and compare them to make sure they are not the same. If the word stems are equal then they are unlikely to be a simplification, so this pair is discarded. Some valid simplifications may also be removed at this point, however these are difficult to distinguish from the non-simplifications.

Synonymy Check

Typically, lexical simplification involves the selection of a word's synonym. WordNet (Fellbaum, 1998) is used as a thesaurus to check if the second word is listed as a synonym of the first. As previously discussed (Section 2.1), we do not take word sense into account at this point. Some valid simplifications may not be identified as synonyms in WordNet, however we choose to take this risk — discarding all non-synonym pairs. Improving thesaurus coverage for complex words is left to future work.

Stemming is favoured over lemmatisation for two reasons. Firstly, because lemmatisation requires a lot of processing power and would have terminally slowed the processing of the large revision histories. Secondly, stemming is a dictionary-independent technique, meaning it can handle any unknown words. Lemmatisation requires a large dictionary, which may not contain the rare CWs which are identified.

Simplicity Check

Finally, we check that the second word is simpler than the first using the SUBTLEX frequencies. All these checks result in a pair of sentences, with one word difference. The differing words are synonyms and the change has been to a word which is simpler than the original. Given these conditions have been met, we store the pair in our CW Corpus as an example of a lexical simplification.

2.3 Examples

This process was used to mine the following two examples:

Complex word: functions.
Simple word: uses.
A dictionary has been designed to have one or more ________ that can help the user in a particular situation.

Complex word: difficult
Simple word: hard
Readability tests give a prediction as to how ________ readers will find a particular text.

3 Corpus Analysis

3.1 Experimental Design

To determine the validity of the CW corpus, a set of six mutually exclusive 50-instance random samples from the corpus were turned into questionnaires. One was given to each of 6 volunteer annotators who were asked to determine, for each sentence, whether it was a true example of a simplification or not. If so, they marked the example as correct. This binary choice was employed to simplify the task for the annotators. A mixture of native and non-native English speakers was used, although no marked difference was observed between these groups. All the annotators are proficient in English and currently engaged in further or higher education. In total, 300 instances of lexical simplification were evaluated, covering over 40% of the CW corpus.

A 20 instance sample was also created as a validation set. The same 20 instances were randomly interspersed among each of the 6 datasets and used to calculate the inter-annotator agreement. The validation data consisted of 10 examples from the CW corpus and 10 examples that were filtered out during the earlier stages of processing. This provided sufficient positive and negative data to show the annotator's understanding of the task. These examples were hand picked to represent positive and negative data and are used as a gold standard.

Agreement with the gold standard is calculated using Cohen's kappa (Cohen, 1968). Inter-annotator agreement is calculated using Fleiss' kappa (Fleiss, 1971), as in the evaluation of a similar task presented in de Belder and Moens (2012). In total, each annotator was presented with 70 examples and asked to label these. A small sample size was used to reduce the effects of annotator fatigue.

Annotation Index	Cohen's Kappa	Sample Accuracy
1	1	98%
2	1	96%
3	0.4	70%
4	1	100%
5	0.6	84%
6	1	96%

Table 2: The results of different annotations. The kappa score is given against the gold standard set of 20 instances. The sample accuracy is the percentage of the 50 instances seen by that annotator which were judged to be true examples of a lexical simplification. Note that kappa is strongly correlated with accuracy (Pearson's correlation: $r = 0.980$)

3.2 Results

Of the six annotations, four show the exact same results on the validation set. These four identify each of the 10 examples from the CW corpus as a valid simplification and each of the 10 examples that were filtered out as an invalid simplification. This is expected as these two sets of data were selected as examples of positive and negative data respectively. The agreement of these four annotators further corroborates the validity of the gold standard. Annotator agreement is shown in Table 2.

The 2 other annotators did not strongly agree on the validation sets. Calculating Cohen's kappa between each of these annotators and the gold standard gives scores of 0.6 and 0.4 respectively, indicating a moderate to low level of agreement. The value for Cohen's kappa between the two non-agreeing annotators is 0.2, indicating that they are in low agreement with each other.

Analysing the errors made by these 2 annotators on the validation set reveals some inconsistencies. E.g., one sentence marked as incorrect changes the fragment 'education and teaching' to 'learning and teaching'. However, every other annotator marked the enclosing sentence as correct. This level of inconsistency and low agreement with the other annotators shows that these annotators had difficulty with the task. They may not have read the instructions carefully or may not have understood the task fully.

Corpus accuracy is defined as the percentage of instances that were marked as being true instances of simplification (not counting those in the validation set). This is out of 50 for each annotator and can be combined linearly across all six annotators.

Taking all six annotators into account, the corpus accuracy is 90.67%. Removing the worst performing annotator (kappa = 0.4) increases the corpus accuracy to 94.80%. If we also remove the next worst performing annotator (kappa = 0.6), leaving us with only the four annotators who were in agreement on the validation set, then the accuracy increases again to 97.5%.

There is a very strong Pearson's correlation ($r = 0.980$) between an annotator's agreement with the gold standard and the accuracy which they give to the corpus. Given that the lower accuracy reported by the non-agreeing annotators is in direct proportion to their deviation from the gold standard, this implies that the reduction is a result of the lower quality of those annotations. Following this, the two non-agreeing annotators should be discounted when evaluating the corpus accuracy — giving a final value of 97.5%.

4 Discussion

The necessity of this corpus developed from a lack of similar resources. CW identification is a hard task, made even more difficult if blind to its evaluation. With this new resource, CW identification becomes much easier to evaluate. The specific target application for this is lexical simplification systems as previously mentioned. By establishing and improving upon the state of the art in CW identification, lexical simplification systems will directly benefit by knowing which wordforms are problematic to a user.

Methodologically, the corpus is simple to use and can be applied to evaluate many current systems (see Section 6). Techniques using distributional semantics (Bott et al., 2012) may require more context than is given by just the sentence. This is a shortcoming of the corpus in its present form, although not many techniques currently require this level of context. If necessary, context vectors may be extracted by processing Simple Wikipedia edit histories (as presented in Section 2.2) and extracting the required information at the appropriate point.

There are 731 lexical edits in the corpus. Each one of these may be used as an example of a complex and a simple word, giving us 1,462 points of data for evaluation. This is larger than a comparable data set for a similar task (de Belder and Moens, 2012). Ways to further increase the number of instances are discussed in Section 6.

It would appear from the analysis of the validation sets (presented above in Section 3.2) that two of the annotators struggled with the task of annotation, attaining a low agreement against the gold standard. This is most likely due to the annotators misunderstanding the task. The annotations were done at the individual's own workstation and the main guidance was in the form of instructions on the questionnaire. These instructions should be updated and clarified in further rounds of annotation. It may be useful to allow annotators direct contact with the person administering the questionnaire. This would allow clarification of the instructions where necessary, as well as helping annotators to stay focussed on the task.

The corpus accuracy of 97.5% implies that there is a small error rate in the corpus. This occurs due to some non-simplifications slipping through the checks. The error rate means that if a system were to identify CWs perfectly, it would only attain 97.5% accuracy on the CW corpus. CW identification is a difficult task and systems are unlikely to have such a high accuracy that this will be an issue. If systems do begin to attain this level of accuracy then a more rigorous corpus will be warranted in future.

There is significant interest in lexical simplification for languages which are not English (Bott et al., 2012; Aluísio and Gasperin, 2010; Dell'Orletta et al., 2011; Keskisärkkä, 2012). The technique for discovering lexical simplifications presented here relies heavily on the existence of Simple English Wikipedia. As no other simplified language Wikipedia exists, it would be very difficult to create a CW corpus for any language other than English. However, the corpus can be used to evaluate CW identification techniques which will be transferrable to other languages, given the existence of sufficient resources.

5 Related Work

As previously noted, there is a systemic lack of evaluation in the literature. Notable exceptions come from the medical domain and include the work of Zeng et al. (2005), Zeng-Treitler et al. (2008) and Elhadad (2006). Zeng et al. (2005) first look at word familiarity scoring correlated against user questionnaires and predictions made by a support vector machine. They show that they are able to predict the complexity of medical terminology with a relative degree of accuracy. This work is continued in Zeng-Treitler et al. (2008), where a word's context is used to predict its familiarity. This is similarly correlated against a user survey and used to show the importance of context in predicting word familiarity. The work of Elhadad (2006) uses frequency and psycholinguistic features to predict term familiarity. They find that the size of their corpus greatly affects their accuracy. Whilst these techniques focus on the medical domain, the research presented in this paper is concerned with the more general task of CW identification in natural language.

There are two standard ways of identifying CWs in lexical simplification systems. Firstly, systems attempt to simplify every word (Devlin and Tait, 1998; Thomas and Anderson, 2012; Bott et al., 2012), assuming that CWs will be modified, but for simple words, no simpler alternative will exist. The danger is that too many simple words may be modified unnecessarily, resulting in a change of meaning. Secondly, systems use a threshold over some word familiarity score (Biran et al., 2011; Elhadad, 2006; Zeng et al., 2005). Word frequency is typically used as the familiarity score, although it may also be combined with word length (Biran et al., 2011). The advent of the CW corpus will allow these techniques to be evaluated alongside each other on a common data set.

The CW corpus is similar in conception to the aforementioned lexical simplification dataset (de Belder and Moens, 2012) which was produced for the SemEval 2012 Task 1 on lexical simplification. This dataset allows synonym ranking systems to be evaluated on the same platform and was highly useful during this research (see Table 1).

6 Future Work

The CW corpus is still relatively small at 731 instances. It may be grown by carrying out the same process with revision histories from the main English Wikipedia. Whilst the English Wikipedia revision histories will have fewer valid simplifications per revision, they are much more extensive and contain a lot more data. As well as growing the CW corpus in size, it would be worthwhile to look at ways to improve its accuracy. One way would be to ask a team of annotators to evaluate every single instance in the corpus and to discard or keep each according to their recommendation.

Experiments using the corpus are presented in Shardlow (2013), further details on the use of the corpus can be found by following this reference. Three common techniques for identifying CWs are implemented and statistically evaluated. The CW Corpus is available from META-SHARE[5] under a CC-BY-SA Licence.

Acknowledgments

This research is supported by EPSRC grant EP/I028099/1. Thanks go to the annotators and reviewers, who graciously volunteered their time.

References

Sandra Maria Aluísio and Caroline Gasperin. 2010. Fostering digital inclusion and accessibility: the PorSimples project for simplification of Portuguese texts. In *Proceedings of the NAACL HLT 2010 Young Investigators Workshop on Computational Approaches to Languages of the Americas*, YIWCALA '10, pages 46–53, Stroudsburg, PA, USA. Association for Computational Linguistics.

Or Biran, Samuel Brody, and Noémie Elhadad. 2011. Putting it simply: a context-aware approach to lexical simplification. In *Proceed-*

[5] http://tinyurl.com/cwcorpus

ings of the 49th Annual Meeting of the Association for Computational Linguistics: Human Language Technologies: short papers - Volume 2, HLT '11, pages 496–501, Stroudsburg, PA, USA. Association for Computational Linguistics.

Stefan Bott, Luz Rello, Biljana Drndarevic, and Horacio Saggion. 2012. Can Spanish be simpler? LexSiS: Lexical simplification for Spanish. In *Coling 2012: The 24th International Conference on Computational Linguistics.*, pages 357–374.

Marc Brysbaert and Boris New. 2009. Moving beyond Kučera and Francis: A critical evaluation of current word frequency norms and the introduction of a new and improved word frequency measure for American English. *Behavior Research Methods*, 41(4):977–990.

Jacob Cohen. 1968. Weighted kappa: nominal scale agreement with provision for scaled disagreement or partial credit. *Psychological Bulletin*, 70(4):213–220.

Jan de Belder and Marie-Francine Moens. 2012. A dataset for the evaluation of lexical simplification. In *Computational Linguistics and Intelligent Text Processing*, volume 7182 of *Lecture Notes in Computer Science*, pages 426–437. Springer, Berlin Heidelberg.

Felice Dell'Orletta, Simonetta Montemagni, and Giulia Venturi. 2011. Read-it: assessing readability of Italian texts with a view to text simplification. In *Proceedings of the Second Workshop on Speech and Language Processing for Assistive Technologies*, SLPAT '11, pages 73–83, Stroudsburg, PA, USA. Association for Computational Linguistics.

Siobhan Devlin and John Tait. 1998. *The use of a psycholinguistic database in the simplification of text for aphasic readers*, volume 77. CSLI Lecture Notes, Stanford, CA: Center for the Study of Language and Information.

Noemie Elhadad. 2006. Comprehending technical texts: Predicting and defining unfamiliar terms. In *AMIA Annual Symposium proceedings*, page 239. American Medical Informatics Association.

Christiane Fellbaum. 1998. *WordNet: An Electronic Lexical Database.* MIT Press, Cambridge, MA.

Joseph L. Fleiss. 1971. Measuring nominal scale agreement among many raters. *Psychological bulletin*, 76:378–382, November.

Robin Keskisärkkä. 2012. Automatic text simplification via synonym replacement. Master's thesis, Linköping University.

Henry Kučera and W. Nelson Francis. 1967. *Computational analysis of present-day American English.* Brown University Press.

Gerard Salton and Chung-Shu Yang. 1973. On the specification of term values in automatic indexing. *Journal of Documentation*, 29(4):351–372.

Matthew Shardlow. 2013. A comparison of techniques to automatically identify complex words. In *Proceedings of the Student Research Workshop at the 51st Annual Meeting of the Association for Computational Linguistics.* Association for Computational Linguistics.

S. Rebecca Thomas and Sven Anderson. 2012. WordNet-based lexical simplification of a document. In *Proceedings of KONVENS 2012*, pages 80–88. ÖGAI, September.

Mark Yatskar, Bo Pang, Cristian Danescu-Niculescu-Mizil, and Lillian Lee. 2010. For the sake of simplicity: unsupervised extraction of lexical simplifications from Wikipedia. In *Human Language Technologies: The 2010 Annual Conference of the North American Chapter of the Association for Computational Linguistics*, HLT '10, pages 365–368, Stroudsburg, PA, USA. Association for Computational Linguistics.

Qing Zeng, Eunjung Kim, Jon Crowell, and Tony Tse. 2005. A text corpora-based estimation of the familiarity of health terminology. In *Biological and Medical Data Analysis*, volume 3745 of *Lecture Notes in Computer Science*, pages 184–192. Springer, Berlin Heidelberg.

Qing Zeng-Treitler, Sergey Goryachev, Tony Tse, Alla Keselman, and Aziz Boxwala. 2008. Estimating consumer familiarity with health terminology: a context-based approach. *Journal of the American Medical Informatics Association*, 15:349–356.

A Pilot Study on Readability Prediction with Reading Time

Hitoshi Nishikawa, Toshiro Makino and **Yoshihiro Matsuo**
NTT Media Intelligence Laboratories, NTT Corporation
1-1 Hikari-no-oka, Yokosuka-shi, Kanagawa, 239-0847 Japan
{nishikawa.hitoshi, makino.toshiro, matsuo.yoshihiro}@lab.ntt.co.jp

Abstract

In this paper we report the results of a pilot study of basing readability prediction on training data annotated with reading time. Although reading time is known to be a good metric for predicting readability, previous work has mainly focused on annotating the training data with subjective readability scores usually on a 1 to 5 scale. Instead of the subjective assessments of complexity, we use the more objective measure of reading time. We create and evaluate a predictor using the binary classification problem; the predictor identifies the better of two documents correctly with 68.55% accuracy. We also report a comparison of predictors based on reading time and on readability scores.

1 Introduction

Several recent studies have attempted to predict the readability of documents (Pitler and Nenkova, 2008; Burstein et al., 2010; Nenkova et al., 2010; Pitler et al., 2010; Tanaka-Ishii et al., 2010). Predicting readability has a very important role in the field of computational linguistics and natural language processing:

- Readability prediction can help users retrieve information from the Internet. If the readability of documents can be predicted, search engines can rank the documents according to readability, allowing users to access the information they need more easily (Tanaka-Ishii et al., 2010).

- The predicted readability of a document can be used as an objective function in natural language applications such as machine translation, automatic summarization, and document simplification. Machine translation can use a readability predictor as a part of the objective function to make more fluent translations (Nenkova et al., 2010). The readability predictor can also be used as a part of a summarizer to generate readable summaries (Pitler et al., 2010). Document simplification can help readers understand documents more easily by automatically rewriting documents that are not easy to read (Zhu et al., 2010; Woodsend and Lapata, 2011). This is possible by paraphrasing the sentences so as to maximize document readability.

- Readability prediction can be used for educational purposes (Burstein et al., 2010). It can assess human-generated documents automatically.

Most studies build a predictor that outputs a readability score (generally 1-5 scale) or a classifier or ranker that identifies which of two documents has the better readability. Using textual complexity to rank documents may be adequate for several applications in the fields of information retrieval, machine translation, document simplification, and the assessment of human-written documents. Approaches based on complexity, however, do not well support document summarization.

In the context of automatic summarization, users want concise summaries to understand the important information present in the documents *as rapidly as possible*— to create summaries that can be read as quickly as possible, we need a function that can evaluate the quality of the summary in terms of reading time.

To achieve this goal, in this paper, we show the results of our pilot study on predicting the reading time of documents. Our predictor has two features as follows:

1. Our predictor is trained by documents directly annotated with reading time. While previous work employs subjective assessments of complexity, we directly use the reading time to build a predictor. As a predictor, we adopt Ranking SVM (Joachims, 2002).

2. The predictor predicts the reading time without recourse to features related to document length since our immediate goal is text summarization. A preliminary experiment confirms that document length is effective for readability prediction confirming the work by (Pitler and Nenkova, 2008; Pitler et al., 2010). Summarization demands that the predictor work well regardless of text length.

This is the first report to show that the result of training a predictor with data annotated by reading time is to improve the quality of automatic readability prediction. Furthermore, we report the result of the comparison between our reading time predictor and a conventional complexity-based predictor.

This paper is organized as follows: Section 2 describes related work. Section 3 describes the data used in the experiments. Section 4 describes our model. Section 5 elaborates the features for predicting document readability based on reading time. Section 6 reports our evaluation experiments. We conclude this paper and show future directions in Section 7.

2 Related Work

Recent work formulates readability prediction as an instance of a classification, regression, or ranking problem. A document is regarded as a mixture of complex features and its readability is predicted by the use of machine learning (Pitler and Nenkova, 2008; Pitler et al., 2010; Tanaka-Ishii et al., 2010). Pitler and Nenkova (2008) built a classifier that employs various features extracted from a document and newswire documents annotated with a readability score on a 1 to 5 scale. They integrated complex features by using SVM and identified the better document correctly with 88.88% accuracy. They reported that the log likelihood of a document based on its discourse relations, the log likelihood of a document based on n-gram, the average number of verb phrases in sentences, the number of words in the document were good indicators on which to base readability prediction. Pitler et al., (2010) used the same framework to predict the linguistic quality of a summary. In the field of automatic summarization, linguistic quality has been assessed manually and hence to automate the assessment is an important research problem (Pitler et al., 2010). A ranker based on Ranking SVM has been constructed (Joachims, 2002) and identified the better of two summaries correctly with an accuracy of around 90%. Tanaka-Ishii et al., (2010) also built a ranker to predict the rank of documents according to readability. While Tanaka-Ishii et al. used word-level features for the prediction, Pitler and Nenkova (2008) and Pitler et al., (2010) also leveraged sentence-level features and document-level features. In this paper, we extend their findings to predict readability. We elaborate our feature set in Section 5. While all of them either classify or rank the documents by assigning a readability score on a 1-5 scale, our research goal is to build a predictor that can also estimate the reading time.

In the context of multi-document summarization, the linguistic quality of a summary is predicted to order the sentences extracted from the original documents (Barzilay and Lapata, 2005; Lapata, 2006; Barzilay and Lapata, 2008). In multi-document summarization, since sentences are extracted from the original documents without regard for context, they must be ordered in some way to make the summary coherent. One of the most important features for ordering sentences is the entity grid suggested by Barzilay and Lapata (2005; 2008). It captures transitions in the semantic roles of the noun phrases in a document, and can predict the quality of an order of the sentences with high accuracy. It was also used as an important feature in the work by Pitler and Nenkova (2008) and Piter et al., (2010) to predict the readability of a document. Burstein et al., (2010) used it for an educational purpose, and used it to predict the readability of essays. Lapata (Lapata, 2006) suggested the use of Kendall's Tau as an indicator of the quality of a set of sentences in particular order; she also reported that self-paced reading time is a good indicator of quality. While Lapata focuses on sentence ordering, our research goal is to predict the overall quality of a document in terms of reading time.

3 Data

To build a predictor that can estimate the reading time of a document, we made a collection of documents and annotated each with its reading time and readability score. We randomly selected 400 articles from Kyoto Text Corpus 4.0 [1]. The corpus consists of newswire articles written in Japanese and annotated with word boundaries, part-of-speech tags and syntactic structures. We developed an experimental system that showed articles for each subject and gathered reading times. Each article was read by 4 subjects. All subjects are native speakers of Japanese.

Basically, we designed our experiment following Pitler and Nenkova (2008). The subjects were asked to use the system to read the articles. They could read each document without a time limit, the only requirement being that they were to understand the content of the document. While the subjects were reading the article, the reading time was recorded by the system. We didn't tell the subjects that the time was being recorded.

To prevent the subjects from only partially reading the document and raise the reliability of the results, we made a multiple-choice question for each document; the answer was to be found in the document. This was used to weed out unreliable results.

After the subjects read the document, they were asked to answer the question.

Finally, the subjects were asked questions related to readability as follows:

1. How well-written is this article?
2. How easy was it to understand?
3. How interesting is this article?

Following the work by Pitler and Nenkova (2008), the subjects answered by selecting a value between 1 and 5, with 5 being the best and 1 being the worst and we used only the answer to the first question (How well-written is this article?) as the readability score. We dropped the results in which the subjects gave the wrong answer to the multiple-choice question. Finally, we had 683 tuples of documents, reading times, and readability scores.

[1] http://nlp.ist.i.kyoto-u.ac.jp/EN/

4 Model

To predict the readability of a document according to reading time, we use Ranking SVM (Joachims, 2002). A target document is converted to a feature vector as explained in Section 5, then the predictor ranks two documents. The predictor assigns a real number to a document as its score; ranking is done according to score. In this paper, a higher score means better readability, i.e., shorter reading time.

5 Features

In this section we elaborate the features used to predict the reading time. While most of them were introduced in previous work, see Section 3, the word level features are introduced here.

5.1 Word-level Features

Character Type (CT)

Japanese sentences consist of several types of characters: kanji, hiragana, katakana, and Roman letters. We use the ratio of the number of kanji to the number of hiragana as a feature of the document.

Word Familiarity (WF)

Amano and Kondo (2007) developed a list of words annotated with word familiarity; it indicates how familiar a word is to Japanese native speakers. The list is the result of a psycholinguistic experiment and the familiarity ranges from 1 to 7, with 7 being the most familiar and 1 being the least familiar. We used the average familiarity of words in the document as a feature.

5.2 Sentence-level Features

Language Likelihood (LL)

Language likelihood based on an n-gram language model is widely used to generate natural sentences. Intuitively, a sentence whose language likelihood is high will have good readability. We made a trigram language model from 17 years (1991-2007) of Mainichi Shinbun Newspapers by using SRILM Toolkit. Since the language model assigns high probability to shorter documents, we normalized the probability by the number of words in a document.

Syntactic Complexity (TH/NB/NC/NP)

Schwarm and Ostendorf (2005) suggested that syntactic complexity of a sentence can be used as a feature for reading level assessment. We use the following features as indicators of syntactic complexity:

- The height of the syntax tree (TH): we use the height of the syntax tree as an indicator of the syntactic complexity of a sentence. Complex syntactic structures demand that readers make an effort to interpret them. We use the average, maximum and minimum heights of syntax trees in a document as a feature.

- The number of bunsetsu (NB): in Japanese dependency parsing, syntactic relations are defined between *bunsetsu*; they are almost the same as Base-NP (Veenstra, 1998) with postpositions. If a sentence has a lot of bunsetsu, it can have a complex syntactic structure. We use the average, maximum and minimum number of them as a feature.

- The number of commas (NC): a comma suggests a complex syntax structure such as subordinate and coordinate clauses. We use the average, maximum and minimum number of them as a feature.

- The number of predicates (NP): intuitively, a sentence can be syntactically complex if it has a lot of predicates. We use the average, maximum and minimum number of them as a feature.

5.3 Document-level Features

Discourse Relations (DR)

Pitler and Nenkova (2008) used discourse relations of the Penn Discourse Treebank (Prasad et al., 2008) as a feature. Since our corpus doesn't have human-annotated discourse relations between the sentences, we use the average number of connectives per sentence as a feature. Intuitively, the explicit discourse relations indicated by the connectives will yield better readability.

Entity Grid (EG)

Along with the previous work (Pitler and Nenkova, 2008; Pitler et al., 2010), we use entity grid (Barzilay and Lapata, 2005; Barzilay and Lapata, 2008) as a feature. We make a vector whose element is the transition probability between syntactic roles (i.e. subject, object and other) of the noun phrases in a document. Since our corpus consists of Japanese documents, we use postpositions to recognize the syntactic role of a noun phrase. Noun phrases with postpositions "Ha" and "Ga" are recognized as subjects. Noun phrases with postpositions "Wo" and "Ni" are recognized as objects. Other noun phrases are marked as other. We combine the entity grid vector to form a final feature vector for predicting reading time.

Lexical Cohesion (LC)

Lexical cohesion is one of the strongest features for predicting the linguistic quality of a summary (Pitler et al., 2010). Following their work, we leverage the cosine similarity of adjacent sentences as a feature. To calculate it, we make a word vector by extracting the content words (nouns, verbs and adjectives) from a sentence. The frequency of each word in the sentence is used as the value of the sentence vector. We use the average, maximum and minimum cosine similarity of the sentences as a feature.

6 Experiments

This section explains the setting of our experiment. As mentioned above, we adopted Ranking SVM as a predictor. Since we had 683 tuples (documents, reading time and readability scores), we made ${}_{683}C_2 = 232,903$ pairs of documents for Ranking SVM. Each pair consists of two documents where one has a shorter reading time than the other. The predictor learned which parameters were better at predicting which document would have the shorter reading time, i.e. higher score. We performed a 10-fold cross validation on the pairs consisting of the reading time explained in Section 3 and the features explained in Section 5. In order to analyze the contribution of each feature

Features	Accuracy
ALL	68.45
TH + EG + LC	**68.55**
Character Type (CT)	52.14
Word Familiarity (WF)	51.30
Language Likelihood (LL)	50.40
Height of Syntax Tree (TH)	61.86
Number of Bunsetsu (NB)	51.54
Number of Commas (NC)	47.07
Number of Predicates (NP)	52.82
Discourse Relations (DR)	48.04
Entity Grid (EG)	67.74
Lexical Cohesion (LC)	61.63
Document Length	69.40
Baseline	50.00

Table 1: Results of proposed reading time predictor.

to prediction accuracy, we adopted a linear kernel. The range of the value of each feature was normalized to lie between -1 and 1.

6.1 Classification based on reading time

Table 1 shows the results yielded by the reading time predictor. ALL indicates the accuracy achieved by the classifier with all features explained in Section 5. At the bottom of Table 1, Baseline shows the accuracy of random classification. As shown in Table 1, since the height of syntax tree, entity grid and lexical cohesion are good indicators for the prediction, we combined these features. TH + EG + LC indicates that this combination achieves the best performance.

As to individual features, most of them couldn't distinguish a better document from a worse one. CT, WF and LL show similar performance to Baseline. The reason why these features failed to clearer identify the better of the pair could be because the documents are newswire articles. The ratio between kanji and hiragana, CT, is similar in most of the articles and hence it couldn't identify the better document. Similarly, there isn't so much of a difference among the documents in terms of word familiarity, WF. The language model used, LL, was not effective against the documents tested but it is expected that it would useful if the target documents came from different fields.

Among the syntactic complexity features, TH offers the best performance. Since its learned feature weight is negative, the result shows that a higher syntax tree causes longer reading time. While TH has shows good performance, NB, NC and NP fail to offer any significant advantage. As with the word-level features, there isn't so much of a difference among the documents in terms of the values of these features. This is likely because most of the newswire articles are written by experts for a restricted field.

Among the document-level features, EG and LC show good performance. While Pitler and Nenkova (2008) have shown that the discourse relation feature is strongest at predicting the linguistic quality of a document, DR shows poor performance. Whereas they modeled the discourse relations by a multinomial distribution using human-annotated labels, DR was simply the number of connectives in the document. A more sophisticated approach will be needed to model discourse.

EG and LC show the best prediction performance of the single features, which agrees with previous work (Pitler and Nenkova, 2008; Pitler et al., 2010). While, as shown above, most of the sentence-level features don't have good discriminative performance, EG and LC work well. Since these features can work well in homogeneous documents like newswire articles, it is reasonable to expect that they will also work well in heterogeneous documents from various domains.

We also show the classification result achieved with document length. Piter and Nenkova (2008) have shown that document length is a strong indicator for readability prediction. We measure document length by three criteria: the number of characters, the number of words and the number of sentences in the document. We used these values as features and built a predictor. While the document length has the strongest classification performance, the predictor with TH + EG + LC shows equivalent performance.

6.2 Classification based on readability score

We also report that the result of the classification based on the readability score in Table 2. Along with the result of the reading time, we tested ALL and TH + EG + LC, and the single features. While DR shows poor classification performance in terms of reading time, it shows the best classi-

Features	Accuracy
ALL	57.25
TH + DR + EG + LC	56.51
TH + EG + LC	56.50
Character Type (CT)	51.96
Word Familiarity (WF)	51.50
Language Likelihood (LL)	50.68
Height of Syntax Tree (TH)	55.77
Number of Bunsetsu (NB)	52.99
Number of Commas (NC)	51.50
Number of Predicates (NP)	52.56
Discourse Relations (DR)	**58.14**
Entity Grid (EG)	56.14
Lexical Cohesion (LC)	55.77
Document Length	56.83
Baseline	50.00

Table 2: A result of classification based on readability score.

	Cor. coef.
Reading Time	0.822
Readability Score	0.445

Table 3: Correlation coefficients of the reading time and readability score between the subjects. We calculated the coefficient for each pair of subjects and then averaged them.

fication performance as regards readability score. Hence we add the result of TH + DR + EG + LC. It agrees with the findings showed by Pitler and Nenkova (2008) in which they have shown discourse relation is the best feature for predicting the readability score.

In general, the same features used for classification based on the reading time work well for predicting the readability score. TH and EG, LC have good prediction performance.

6.3 Variation in reading time vs. variation in readability score

We show the correlation between the subjects in terms of the variation in reading time and readability score in Table 3. As shown, the reading time shows much higher correlation (less variation) than the readability score. This agrees with the findings shown by Lapata (2006) in which the reading time is a better indicator for readability prediction. Since the readability score varies widely among the subjects, training becomes problematic with lowers predictor performance.

The biggest difference between the prediction of the reading time and readability score is the effect of feature DR. One hypothesis that could explain the difference is that the use of connectives works as a strong sign that the document has a good readability score—it doesn't necessarily imply that the document has good *readability*—for the subjects. That is, the subjects perceived the documents with more connectives as readable, however, those connectives contribute to the reading time. Of course, our feature about discourse relations is just based on their usage frequency and hence more precise modeling could improve performance.

7 Conclusion and Future Work

This paper has described our pilot study of readability prediction based on reading time. With automatic summarization in mind, we built a predictor that can predict the reading time, and readability, of a document. Our predictor identified the better of two documents with 68.55% accuracy without using features related to document length.

The following findings can be extracted from the results described above:

- The time taken to read documents can be predicted through existing machine learning technique and the features extracted from training data annotated with reading time (Pitler and Nenkova, 2008; Pitler et al., 2010).

- As Lapata (2006) has shown, reading time is a highly effective indicator of readability. In our experiment, reading time showed good agreement among the subjects and hence more coherent prediction results can be expected.

Future work must proceed in many directions:

1. Measuring more precise reading time is one important problem. One solution is to use an eye tracker; it can measure the reading time more accurately because it can capture when

the subject finishes reading a document. In order to prepare the data used in this paper, we set questions so as to identify and drop unreliable data. The eye tracker could alleviate this effort.

2. Testing the predictor in another domain is necessary for creating practical applications. We tested the predictor only in the domain of newswire articles, as described earlier, and different results might be recorded in domains other than newswire articles.

3. Improving the accuracy of the predictor is also important. There could be other features associated with readability prediction. We plan to explore other features.

4. Applying the predictor to natural language generation tasks is particularly important. We plan to integrate our predictor into a summarizer and evaluate its performance.

References

Shigeaki Amano and Tadahisa Kondo. 2007. Reliability of familiarity rating of ordinary japanese words for different years and places. *Behavior Research Methods*, 39(4):1008–1011.

Regina Barzilay and Mirella Lapata. 2005. Modeling local coherence: an entity-based approach. In *Proceedings of the 43rd Annual Meeting on Association for Computational Linguistics (ACL)*, pages 141–148.

Regina Barzilay and Mirella Lapata. 2008. Modeling local coherence: An entity-based approach. *Computational Linguistics*, 34(1):1–34.

Jill Burstein, Joel Tetreault, and Slava Andreyev. 2010. Using entity-based features to model coherence in student essays. In *Proceedings of Human Language Technologies: The 2010 Annual Conference of the North American Chapter of the Association for Computational Linguistics (NAACL-HLT)*, pages 681–684.

Thorsten Joachims. 2002. Optimizing search engines using clickthrough data. In *Proceedings of the ACM Conference on Knowledge Discovery and Data Mining (KDD)*, pages 133–142.

Mirella Lapata. 2006. Automatic evaluation of information ordering: Kendall's tau. *Computational Linguistics*, 32(4):471–484.

Ani Nenkova, Jieun Chae, Annie Louis, and Emily Pitler. 2010. Structural features for predicting the linguistic quality of text: Applications to machine translation, automatic summarization and human-authored text. In Emiel Krahmer and Theunem Mariet, editors, *Empirical Methods in Natural Language Generation: Data-oriented Methods and Empirical Evaluation*, pages 222–241. Springer.

Emily Pitler and Ani Nenkova. 2008. Revisiting readability: A unified framework for predicting text quality. In *Proceedings of the 2008 Conference on Empirical Methods in Natural Language Processing*, pages 186–195.

Emily Pitler, Annie Louis, and Ani Nenkova. 2010. Automatic evaluation of linguistic quality in multi-document summarization. In *Proceedings of the 48th Annual Meeting of the Association for Computational Linguistics*, pages 544–554.

Rashmi Prasad, Nikhil Dinesh, Alan Lee, Eleni Miltsakaki, Livio Robaldo, Aravind Joshi, and Bonnie Webber. 2008. The penn discourse treebank 2.0. In *Proceedings of the 6th International Conference on Language Resources and Evaluation (LREC)*.

Sarah Schwarm and Mari Ostendorf. 2005. Reading level assessment using support vector machines and statistical language models. In *Proceedings of the 43rd Annual Meeting of the Association for Computational Linguistics (ACL)*, pages 523–530.

Kumiko Tanaka-Ishii, Satoshi Tezuka, and Hiroshi Terada. 2010. Sorting by readability. *Computational Linguistics*, 36(2):203–227.

Jorn Veenstra. 1998. Fast np chunking using memory-based learning techniques. In *Proceedings of the 8th Belgian-Dutch Conference on Machine Learning (Benelearn)*, pages 71–78.

Kristian Woodsend and Mirella Lapata. 2011. Learning to simplify sentences with quasi-synchronous grammar and integer programming. In *Proceedings of the 2011 Conference on Empirical Methods in Natural Language Processing (EMNLP)*, pages 409–420.

Zhemin Zhu, Delphine Bernhard, and Iryna Gurevych. 2010. A monolingual tree-based translation model for sentence simplification. In *Proceedings of the 23rd International Conference on Computational Linguistics (Coling 2010)*, pages 1353–1361.

Author Index